A FATHER SHARES

A FATHER SHARES

How to Enrich Family Life

Ralph Bugg

BAKER BOOK HOUSE
Grand Rapids, Michigan

ISBN: 0-8010-0776-3

Printed in the United States of America

Acknowledgments

Quotations without citation were obtained through personal correspondence or interviews.

All Scripture references are from the Revised Standard Version of the Bible, copyrighted 1946, 1952, 1971, 1973.

The author expresses appreciation to the copyright holders for permission to reprint portions of the materials listed:

James Atwater, "Jenny and Beth: A Father Reflects on the Wonder of Daughters," *Today's Health*, May 1975, p. 42. Used with permission *Today's Health* Magazine 1975 ©. All rights reserved.

T. Berry Brazelton, "What Makes a Good Father," *Redbook*, June 1970, p. 74. Copyright 1970 The Redbook Publishing Company. Used by permission.

C. William Chilman, "If I Had Another Chance at Fatherhood," *Today's Health*, April 1969, p. 56. Used with permission *Today's Health* Magazine 1969 ©. All rights reserved.

Eliot A. Daley, "I'd Rather Be a Father," *Reader's Digest*, June 1978, p. 205. Condensed from *Father Feelings* by Eliot A. Daley (Morrow), © 1977 by Eliot A. Daley. Used by permission of William Morrow & Co., Inc.

Lester David, "Mike Douglas: His Common-Sense Views on Sex, Love and Marriage," *Good Housekeeping*, March 1975. © 1975 by the Hearst Corporation. Used by permission.

Otto Friedrich, "Passing on the Torch," *McCall's*, Sept. 1972, p. 20. Used by permission of the McCall Publishing Company.

Margaret Hennig and Anne Jardim, *The Managerial Woman* (Anchor/Doubleday), p. 78. Copyright 1976, 1977 by Margaret Hennig and Anne Jardim. Used by permission.

Murray Kappelman, "At His Own Rate... in His Own Time," *Family HEALTH*, Feb. 1972, p. 16. Used with permission *Family HEALTH* Magazine 1972 ©. All rights reserved.

My thanks go to Marian G. Lord for her editorial consultation and to Dan Van't Kerkhoff of Baker Book House for his attentiveness, enthusiasm, and support.

FOR
Barbara, Randy, Larry, Jennifer
Harold, Flo
Jake, Jody, and Amy

Contents

A Father Shares...

Whenever the six-turned-eleven of us get together, someone is sure to ask, "Remember when...?" When we trapped a monkey in our back yard. When a coastal storm popped the braces on our tent-trailer. When Larry kicked off a shoe and broke his aquarium, and we rushed to scoop up guppies, tetras, and angels. When Jennifer sold six thousand candy bars to finance her gymnastics trips. When we took a puppy to the "dog doctor" and Randy was vexed to find a man—not a canine—wearing the white coat. When Barbara left for college, but I kept setting six places at the table.

This book, which is my way of celebrating being a father, depicts my interactions with my family in good times and bad. On occasions when I feel I know best, I step boldly to the center to lead; at other times I struggle just to hang in there. Things usually work out better than expected: dreaded eventualities fail to materialize and the children prove more dependable and considerate than they seemed.

I admire the way John F. Kennedy openly relished being President (none of that "poor, overburdened me" stuff), and I advocate the same unabashed zest for parenthood. It grieves me to hear parents play games of one-*down*manship, vying to see who can claim the most wretched treatment at the hands of their children—hardly an exercise in faith and love. And I hate to hear a father or mother wish to leapfrog time ("I'll be glad when they're older") or to freeze time ("I dread the day when they'll be teenagers"). Watching children grow is exciting, and each age presents special delights. Jo and I have enjoyed our four children through all those notorious stages and on into young adulthood.

Although our children are doing well, I don't want to characterize this as a "success" story. That would emphasize the destination and its security rather than the journey, where life's deeper meaning lies. What, after all, is success? Is a father more deserving for grooming a perennial winner than for being supportive of a child who is always struggling with the system? I have done some of both, and yet I can't be smug. Too much credit goes to the children themselves, to Jo, and to relatives and friends.

In the winner's circle, a jockey was asked if he had intended to drop back so far before bolting ahead. "Was that where you wanted to be?" Well, he said laconically, that was where the *horse* wanted to be. If I were starting over, I would give my children freer rein—more often let them find their own place, set their own pace. Oh, we would still have rules (a lot of "parent" remains in me), but I would waste less energy trying to manage their time, the length of their hair, the vernacular of their friends, and their bickering with one another. I would push basic goodness more, competitive achievements less, and resist the temptation to withhold acceptance and affection as a penalty for infractions. I would listen to, and enjoy, the harmony of our family song instead of straining to detect muffed notes.

I would encourage the children to appreciate their uniqueness and infinite possibilities, and less often attempt to remake them in my own image. If I had designed them, they would have been four peas in a pod and not nearly so much fun as a green pea, a garbanzo, a black-eye, and a lima bean. Also, I would have forfeited those engaging riddles: How come in the very same family one little boy is quiet, the other boisterous? And why does a daughter whose life is so orderly have a room so messy?

They are different, yet alike. Each is honest, friendly, caring, and productive. Each is guided and bolstered by a vibrant faith.

I'm proud of my children, but as I said earlier, I have had a lot going for me as a father. I haven't had to manage parenthood without a spouse—or with one who was a liability. For several years after I quit a regular job to become a free-lance writer, we had poverty-level income but we managed and things improved. Our children were born strong and complete, and we have all enjoyed health. None of the kids presented us with one of those terrible problems—premarital pregnancy, drug or alcohol abuse, or a desperate act of defiance. None ran away (there were threats, but the little fellows backed down when we offered to lend them a blanket against the cold night) or joined an objectionable community.

Families come in varied configurations, and none is typical anymore. Yet, it seems to me that many of the principles that enrich family life are universal in application. This book is inspired by my own experience, so it is authentic. I borrow from experts, and to that extent it is authoritative. But it is not an attempt to prescribe. You and your family are unique, and you are more capable of adapting what I say to fit your situation than I am capable of telling you precisely what you should do and how. There are already too many "formula" books that deal in pat answers. Dr. Benjamin Spock says, "Parents should never be urged to rear their children in any way that appears to differ appreciably from what they believe in, since that would only create conflict and guilt and impair rather than aid their effectiveness."[1] Besides, some of our best moments of sharing aren't calculated, but spontaneous.

My life has been enriched by individuals who dared to share with me out of their experience, and the insights and inspiration that I have gained encourage me to venture openness and honesty with you. Much of my material is personal, but I have taken pains to avoid the pitfalls of inappropriate invasion of family privacy (Jo and the children have reviewed the manuscript) and embarrassment to the reader. I have attempted to present a context in which the reader can identify with each of us and participate rather than stand apart, a reluctant spectator.

Although I address fathers directly, I believe the book will help mothers to be better parents and more understanding wives. If the nation's mothers were asked what they want most for their families, many would say, "For my husband to spend more time with our children and exercise greater patience." These are central themes in my book, and I suspect I will have some help getting it into male hands.

Once, touring the Paramount Studios in Hollywood with fellow newsmen, I stood in the familiar Western street where scores of tough guys had been gunned down. As we walked past the fake fronts of the saloon, marshal's office, and bank, our guide picked up an odd-looking nail and showed it to us. Half an inch down the shank was a second head that kept the nail from driving in all the way, ensuring room for the claws of a wrecking hammer. "This nail," said our host, "is the perfect symbol of Hollywood. Everything is temporary."

Our family isn't like that. We built it to last. We are closely knit and mutually supportive; we enjoy being together; we care for one another. We share a glorious past, an exciting present, and a promising future.

Thank you, God, for letting Jo and the children be part of me, and I them. And thanks for five extra blessings: a superb son-in-law, a marvelous daughter-in-law, and three wonderful grandchildren to keep us young and pliable.

NOTE

[1]Spock, "Don't Blame Me," *Look*, Jan. 26, 1971, p. 37.

If Only
I Had
the Time!

1

Nursing my second cup of coffee, I eased down onto the front stoop beside Jennifer, who was waiting for the school bus. A mockingbird singing atop a utility pole caught our attention. Now and then it interrupted its warbling to flash into the air and issue shrill cries. Soon we were asking our favorite question: "Why?" Jennifer suggested the bird was either hungry or calling its mate. I said it might be warning, "This is my territory, keep out!" Or was the creature simply celebrating being alive?

We didn't reach a conclusion. The big, yellow bus appeared and off Jennifer ran. I waved goodbye and went inside feeling good. Ten minutes with my daughter had gotten my day off to a bright start.

Jennifer is our fourth child, which means I had three others to practice on. One thing I learned was to grab moments for sharing whenever I could.

Back when I was night city editor of the *Atlanta Constitution*, I worked until 2 a.m. Coming home to a deathly quiet house, I would have a sandwich, then go upstairs and undress and slip under the covers with Jo. My nudges, flounces, and coughs rarely awakened her. Those were lonely times.

Then Jennifer came along and I had myself a drinking buddy. She required a wee-hours bottle and I gave it to her. In time we graduated to milk and crackers and conversation about things that may interest a little lady and her father. Our tea party concluded, I would take her back upstairs, plop her into her bed, and tell her soothing stories about a little yellow bird who became very, very sleepy. And with her father tousling her hair and rubbing her back, the little girl in the yellow pajamas grew very, very sleepy, too.

My late-night schedule gave rise to another ritual. Mornings at ten, Jo, Larry, and Jennifer served me breakfast in bed. We chatted while I ate, then cleared the dishes for a romp. The children struggled to pin me down, and I delighted them with ferris-wheel rides aboard my outstretched feet. These were fun times—I know because Larry was a connoiseur of pleasurable events, and he never let other activities interfere. After the roughhousing, we sometimes gathered the neighborhood preschoolers and drove to a nearby park for a picnic and more play.

Later, with all four children in school, time for sharing was harder to come by. I was asleep when they left, and home just an hour or so after they returned. Our only shared meal was at 5 p.m. Having to come in from play vexed the children, and with me intent upon getting off to work at a job I had come to hate, our togetherness was strained. Weekends were mitigating interludes but they could not make up for the gaps. Additionally, Jo

A Father Shares

was having to act as both mother and father, coping with the children's homework, schedules, money concerns, and disputes. After they were in bed, she would be alone to think and feel uneasy without me. Meanwhile, I felt guilty over my absence. I feared I was becoming an outsider.

One afternoon, Jo broke down and cried, and that night I asked my boss for day work. I didn't get it, and the refusal heightened my discontent. I had been with the paper twelve years and felt I deserved some consideration. A year later, for accumulated reasons, I quit.

I began a new career as a free-lance writer, which gave me plenty of time to be with my family, although less money than before. I no longer needed that classic lament of fathers: "If only I had the time!" That expression implies a fond hope that someone will make time for us—magically, as the little elves made shoes at night for the poor cobbler and his wife. No one, of course, can make time; we can only make decisions about how we will use the time that we have. Too often we look to some idealized future that promises large blocks of time for sharing. While we await it, the clock hands twirl and calendar pages crumple; the fancy dollhouse and nifty playroom go unbuilt; and the grand western tour and wilderness canoe trip remain mere finger-tracings on maps.

Time ran out for a father and son whom I'll call Henry and Richard. In his early teens, Henry lost an arm in an automobile accident, eclipsing his aspiration to be a football star. Later, he hoped that he and his wife would have a son to fulfill the lost dream. They had two daughters—pretty and smart, but girls nonetheless. Then Richard arrived. Cheers! Alas, Richard wanted to play, not football, but the piano, a preference that brought ridicule from the father. In time, exchanges of curt reprimands and sullen rebellion created a combative atmosphere, and when Richard, in his late teens, took on the "hippie" accouterments of long hair and guitar, Henry issued an ultimatum: "Cut that hair or get out!" Richard got out, and soon he was bumming around Europe.

Privately, father and son indicated they cared for each other and expected time to heal their estrangement. But while Richard was overseas, his father died of electrocution in the plant where he worked. For a decade now, Richard has suffered severe emotional problems. He cannot sort out the tangle of feelings of affection, anger, guilt, regret. He's a drifter, unable to hold onto a job.

"Tell me about my father," he entreats relatives and friends. "I didn't know him very well. I wish we could have been closer."

Time is elusive. It's as though your child cried out, "Daddy, come quick," but you didn't get there, and childhood slipped away. Left behind are artifacts, including photographs of a bright-faced boy or girl that you meant to get close to, but didn't.

Often, attitude determines success or failure. I recall a flight home to Atlanta during which the captain announced a delay. My seat mate whacked his magazine against his knee and complained: "Why does it always happen on Friday nights? My son is playing his first varsity basketball game and he's going to be awfully disappointed. My wife says the kids are growing up without knowing their father. I try to make it up to them on weekends, but it's impossible. A day contains only twenty-four hours no matter how you slice it. As long as I'm a salesman, I'm doomed to be a poor husband and father."

I related this sad story to a friend, a salesman who is away most of the week. "Yeah," he said, "Fridays are bad because the pressure has been building.

You're tired of restaurant food, living out of a suitcase, being surrounded by strangers, and placating ornery customers. You want to get home, relax, have a good meal, be with your family, sleep in your own bed. If something happens, you lose your cool.

"But every job has its demands, right? I like mine and I'm good at it. Sure, I miss my family and they miss me," he said, "but we have talked about it, and as long as I'm happy, they want me to keep doing what I'm doing. The other guy defeats himself when he says that a day has only twenty-four hours no matter how you slice it, because how you slice it makes all the difference in the world. My family and I don't focus on the time we *don't* have, but on the time we do have. I call home, write the kids individually. On weekends, we do fun things together, and I take extra time off in conjunction with holidays. Every summer, we take a long trip. In spite of our limitations, we have remained close."

In contrast, many families are crushed by occupational demands laid upon the father—demands that seem antisocial and inhumane. A young father who had been interviewed by a big corporation said the chief executive told him: "We demand total commitment—not 99 percent, but 100 percent. When you work for us, your family has to be subordinate. And we believe that our salaries are commensurate with this expectation." Such enforced loyalty may escalate sales; unfortunately, it has the same effect on divorce rates and juvenile delinquency.

The owner of a motel chain, who himself works an eighty-hour week, told a graduating class, "A man can never be successful until he teaches his wife not to expect him home for dinner." But Alfred Messer, a family psychiatrist in Atlanta, asks, "After twelve or fourteen hours on the job, what's left

If Only I Had the Time!   21

for a man's family? Many companies give their automobiles and airplanes better treatment than they give their employees. Maybe a father ought to get a high mark not only for his sales but also for attending his child's graduation exercise."

Having chided employers, let me acknowledge that many men voluntarily subordinate their families to their work. Korczak Ziolkowski, who is cutting a gigantic figure of Chief Crazy Horse in a Black Hills mountainside, declared on national television that the sculpture comes ahead of his wife and children.[1] His declaration jarred me, but I realize that thousands of men are putting their work ahead of their families every day, if less blatantly than Ziolkowski. At least the sculptor was honest and told his bride-to-be it would be this way.

In some families that I know, the most significant father-child communication of the day goes something like this:

"Dad, can I have the car tonight?"

"No. I told you last week that if you didn't keep the lawn trimmed I was going to cut back on your privileges."

"Aw, dad!" (Son exits. Father resumes reading newspaper. Curtain.)

I want to believe that this half-minute exchange doesn't represent calculated value, but husbands and fathers can be obstinately stingy with their time. Alex Haley, author of *Roots*, says that during the first of his two failed marriages, he became obsessed with writing. His wife confronted him: "You've got to choose between me and that typewriter."

"I just kept on typing," Haley relates.[2]

Overzealousness put tremendous pressure upon the family of Dan Rather, now co-editor of CBS Television's "60 Minutes." He accepted a succession of transfers which caused his daughter to attend four different schools in the first grade.

"We were a young couple and trying to make it. We ought to have known better but we didn't," Rather said in an interview with Peter A. Janssen, published in *Parents*. He was chasing the "big story" (civil rights at that time). "I should have stopped and said, 'If that is what it takes, I won't do it.' But I didn't do that." (He would have been granted time off had he asked for it, he acknowledges.)

Son and daughter have turned out fine, Rather says, adding, "We were lucky."[3]

Another television personality, Phil Donahue, is a self-acknowledged workaholic. His sixteen-year marriage ended in divorce, and his sons live with him, his daughter with her mother. He says he is attempting "to make it up to the children for all the toys I didn't repair when I had 'more important' things on my mind." Now he monitors his schedule to ensure time for the children. "We have a very close relationship," he says.[4]

"Success" doesn't necessarily wreck family life. George Vaillant, Harvard University psychiatrist, found a correlation between career achievement and family closeness.[5] But ambition's tugs are alluring, and it takes firm resolve to protect family interests. In *Father Feelings*, Eliot A. Daley— minister, former teacher, and currently a writer for the "Mister Rogers' Neighborhood" television program—describes being pulled this way and that:

> I continue to chart my worth by beacons and landmarks set out by average men. . . . How can I sweep away all that average clutter? . . . I mean, what have I done in my whole life that was any more significant than fathering three human beings? Once they didn't exist; now they live. They hurt and heal and

love and laugh; they make mistakes and weave magic; they will bring children into the world, and celebrate and mourn. . . . That counts. Ultimately, I know it does, and I am determined to give my fathering its due. But I can't help wishing for some help, something we men could do to support each other. . . . [6]

* * *

Nurturing both career and family requires resourcefulness and effort. When Mike Douglas was touring with bands, his wife, Gen, was left alone back home with the infant twins, and many nights she cried herself to sleep. In an interview with Lester David, published in *Good Housekeeping*, the talk-show host recalls:

One day I returned home and we reached a big decision. We agreed that from then on, no matter what, we would manage to stay together as a family. And we did. Somehow, we always were able to come up with enough money. I can't tell you how often we were together in a single hotel room, filled with babies, bottles and diapers. I'm certain the fact that we made the effort to remain together was the main reason our marriage has lasted. I believe love thrives on mutual respect and understanding, on the ability to give yourself to another person, and on the capacity of two people to grow together.[7]

I have discussed several reasons why fathers shortchange their families. Here are additional reasons:

We fail to recognize our importance and capabilities. We are conditioned to minimize our value and doubt our potential, and sometimes we take refuge in our maleness. But the father role, long neglected by researchers as by the general public, is now receiving attention. In "A New Look at Life with Father" in the *New York Times Magazine*, Glenn

Collins reports that the consensus of the researchers is that fathers are both important and
capable. He quotes Henry Biller, professor of psychology, University of Rhode Island:

> The presence and availability of fathers to kids is
> critical to their knowledge of social reality, their
> ability to relate to male figures, to their self-
> concepts, their acceptance of their own sexuality,
> their feelings of security. Fathers are important in
> the first years of life, and important throughout a
> child's development.[8]

In a study of middle-class adolescents, Dr. Urie
Bronfenbrenner, professor of human development
and psychology, Cornell University, found prolonged parental absences to have profound effects:

> Children who reported that their parents were
> away from home for long periods of time rated
> significantly lower on such characteristics as re-
> sponsibility and leadership. Perhaps because it was
> more pronounced, absence of the father was more
> critical than that of the mother, particularly in its
> effect on boys. In general, father absence contrib-
> utes to low motivation for achievement, inability to
> defer immediate rewards for later benefits, low
> self-esteem, susceptibility to group influences and
> juvenile delinquency.[9]

Father absenteeism can have lasting effects.
Asked why he had not married, the late United
Nations secretary-general, Dag Hammarskjöld, replied that he had watched his mother suffer from
his father's absences on public business, and he
didn't want to subject another woman to such a life.

In his *New York Times Magazine* article, Collins
paints a positive picture of fatherhood potential. He
reports that the consensus of social scientists involved in pertinent research is that children attach
themselves to fathers as readily as they do to

mothers, and dads have the potential to be protective and giving and to be good caretakers. There is a bonus: fathers relate to children in distinctive ways as well as in the ways that mothers do.[10]

Researchers say that *while* parenting, fathers do well—trouble is, they aren't in the role often enough or for long enough periods of time. We have the potential, we just don't fulfill it.

We focus on the grand and forfeit the obvious. We count on bonanzas which, even if they materialize, may not fulfill our expectations. Several weeks spent in the mountains or at the seashore have distinct advantages—for example, you have time to slow to a leisurely pace and shuck "father-knows-best" attitudes. But dream vacations aren't essential. What holds our lives together are those brief, intermittent episodes of sharing: a game of pitch before supper; a bedtime story and prayer; a chat with a youngster home from a date; a cheery greeting and a pat on the back; a silent glance that says, "I love you." These mini-exchanges are instantly available and require little effort; yet we pass them up.

We have a crisis orientation. As a people, we blink at air pollution until a stagnating inversion chokes us; we dismiss reports of gasoline shortages until we find ourselves lined up at the pumps; and we take our children for granted until they jar us with an act of defiance—or become ill—or simply grow up.

A young minister who was married to the church and parent to the parish came home one night to find the parsonage dark and forlorn. Attached to his pillow was this note: "When you agree to give me and the children one day a week—just one measly day, mind you—we'll come back, but not until you promise."

"I promised!" he said. "I saw I'd been playing games with myself. God put us in families as part of his purpose, but I was stumbling over my own kids, who desperately needed me, as I rushed out the door to save souls who weren't always receptive. Actually, allowing time for my family has helped my ministry. I'm not weighted down with guilt over feeding the world while starving my family."

We succumb to defeatism. The salesman on the plane let the seeming enormity of his responsibilities and his disappointment over failures demoralize him. Despair is a poor position from which to operate.

If you, too, are discouraged, take heart. You *can* be a better father. You *can* avoid those traps. Assign your family a higher priority; don't wait for the dream vacation at the end of the rainbow; don't doze until a crisis strikes; don't resign to sorry-for-myself feelings.

You *can* share with your family if you'll be as persistent and resourceful in managing family time as you are in managing work time. The trick is to start *now,* whatever your circumstances. Begin by setting one or two reasonable and well-defined goals. Examples: "I will come home thirty minutes earlier on Wednesdays." "I will accompany my family to Sunday school this week." "On my next fishing trip, instead of taking one of the fellows, I'll take my kids."

Staying in touch requires effort. Dave Michaels, news anchor for an Atlanta television station, drives home following the evening show and enjoys a dinner break with his family, then returns to the station to prepare for the 11 o'clock show.[11] Stuart Eizenstat, adviser to President Carter, is similarly committed to dinner with his wife and sons. Although he is described as intense and disciplined on the job, he has been known to leave an ongoing meeting with the President at 6:30 rather than keep his wife and children waiting.[12]

Here are ways other fathers manage. The father:

• plays with his toddler before leaving for work.

• takes his daughter on an annual long-weekend "vacation." They stay in a hotel, eat in restaurants, see the sights.

• drives as his son throws papers on Sunday mornings.

• telephones his children during supper breaks.

• watches television cartoons with his young daughter Saturday mornings. "I can screen what she watches, and we discuss things that interest us."

Here are some additional helps:

• Inventory your time. How much free time do you have? How are you spending it? Are you letting discretionary time evaporate simply because you fail to recognize it?

• Organize your work. Some fathers discharge their duties with dispatch and capture time for their families. In contrast, a friend dawdles and then tries to catch up at night. His complaining of overwork further detracts from sharing.

• Weigh your options. Ask yourself: "What would happen if I declined the next promotion? Said no to some overtime? Got somebody else to give the report (or make the trip)?" The consequences may not be all that dire, so why not broach the idea or simply give the change a try?

• Curb intrusions. Discourage business calls at home. Take the phone off the hook during meals, story time, and the like. Some college students praised a professor who permitted calls at home but criticized another who said his off-hours belonged to his family. I suggested they were flunking the wrong teacher.

• Reevaluate community responsibilities. Your most important community is your family. Being a scoutmaster or member of the school board is ordinarily commendable, but not if these duties leave you no time for your own children.

• Share your leisure. Seek out activities that are mutually enjoyable, and you'll more likely engage in them.

• Show and tell. Have your child visit your place of work. He'll better understand what you do and will appreciate where his bread and butter and allowance come from.

• Team up for chores. Although at the time they resisted conscription, my children fondly recall raking leaves and jumping into big piles. Solicit help when you wash the car or prepare breakfast for mom. It may take patience, but remember: once your child becomes proficient, he or she won't need your tutelage and may not seek your company.

• Be together separately. Each child should be an "only" child now and then. Reserve special times for just the two of you and let the child suggest what you'll do.

• Pay attention. Your physical presence of itself can be reassuring, but your undivided attention is a special gift. Also, your child may prefer two minutes when *he* wants it to twenty minutes of your choosing.

• Encourage reciprocation. If your family has a call on your time, you have a right to ask them to share with you and with one another. Some families (notably the Mormons) reserve one night a week for their own sharing and either discourage or prohibit intrusions and excursions.

For balance, here are some cautionary notes. Do not dominate your child's life and smother him in cloying togetherness. Sometimes (if rarely) a father will crowd out peer relationships, causing over-dependency. The ideal is for father and child to walk together, sometimes in each other's shoes, but not in each other's skin.

We need to alternate between companionship and solitude, and sensitive parents will detect times when the child wants privacy. On seashore vacations, Randy climbed into the vacated lifeguard's perch and looked out upon the heaving ocean until darkness shrouded him. What was he thinking about? We never asked. The rest of us cavorted on the beach and left him to his musings.

Some parents seek a more intense relationship than the child wants or can tolerate. Moreover, moods shift, and while a father is wanting closeness, the child may be preoccupied. Rebuffed, the father may feel jealous or unworthy—hardly the appropriate response for a simple problem of timing. The father who, after reading this, feels enthusiastic and moves closer to his daughter or son may experience disinterest, surprise, or even confusion at the sudden turn of events. Be patient and philosophical.

Fathers have deserving needs of their own apart from their children and shouldn't consign themselves to martyrdom. Wives, too, need attention, companionship, and solitude apart from the children.

Although young children have hazy concepts of time, they need practice in deferring gratification. I'm not suggesting you do this arbitrarily, but you might suggest, "Let me rest a while and change into some old clothes and then see what's wrong with your truck." Children can learn to "stretch" time through anticipation of promised treats and remembrance of pleasant experiences.

Tone is important—a sense of duty will show. Family members prefer to feel important and loved. A wife complained, "I would settle for one-tenth of his time if it could be a fresh tenth, but the children and I get the weary, cross, leave-me-alone crumbs."

Time and *family*—both are precious gifts to be nurtured, enjoyed, and celebrated. "This is the day which the Lord has made; let us rejoice and be glad in it" (Ps. 118:24).

NOTES

[1]"60 Minutes," Columbia Broadcasting System.

[2]Interview with Al Martinez, *Los Angeles Times*, in *Atlanta Journal and Constitution* ("Haley Bewildered at Book Impact"), Dec. 19, 1976, p. 32D.

[3]Peter A. Janssen, "Dan Rather: Did His Family Pay for His Success?" *Parents*, Aug. 1978, p. 50.

[4]"Donahue," syndicated television program.

[5]Arthur J. Snider, *Chicago Daily News*, in *Atlanta Constitution* ("Successful Men Make Good Fathers"), May 18, 1976.

[6]See Acknowledgments.

[7]See Acknowledgments.

[8]Glenn Collins, "A New Look at Life with Father," *New York Times Magazine*, June 17, 1979, p. 30.

[9]Urie Bronfenbrenner, "Parents Bring Up Your Children!" *Look*, Jan. 26, 1971, p. 45. Excerpted from *Two Worlds of Childhood: U.S. and U.S.S.R.* (Russell Sage Foundation, 1970).

[10]Collins, "A New Look," p. 30.

[11]Jeff Denberg, "Dave Michaels Happy He's (11) Alive," *Atlanta Journal*, March 27, 1979, p. 1B.

[12]Andrew J. Glass, "Stu Eizenstat—Quiet But Powerful," *Atlanta Journal and Constitution*, June 5, 1977.

It's the Quality
That Counts

2

Early morning in camp! Shafts of sunlight stab through the haze that clings to the mountains and spills down the slopes into our valley. The brisk air carries whiffs of burning oak and perking coffee. The hush is broken only by the chirping of birds foraging for breakfast. This is a new day to be filled with good things.

Uh-oh! That family across the way is stirring. The father shouts, the boy yells back, the mother scolds the two of them, the baby cries. Alas, it seems our new day will be filled with the same angry confrontations that ruined yesterday. Our neighbors would be better off back home, where they would have more buffer space and more diversions. True togetherness is alien to them, and being cramped into a tent and campsite intensifies their antagonisms.

"The family that plays together stays together."

A Father Shares

The recreationists promise this as glibly as the religionists pledge that "The family that *prays* together stays together." But activity isn't a miracle element: *doing* isn't as important as *being*. And togetherness must go beyond geographical proximity. Seizing time for sharing is only a first step, because time of itself lacks meaning; time is merely a medium in which things—good *and* bad—happen. In the last chapter I stressed time. Now I want to emphasize quality.

Back in 1966, when "generation gap" had just been coined and communication had just been invented (or so it seemed), I participated in a family-life conference. Our panel discussed a play that portrayed a splintered family. Repeatedly, we diagnosed their problem as failure to communicate, but then it struck me: they communicated all too well. The fault lay in *what* they communicated. Their values were skewed and they lacked commitment, and so their exchanges were shallow, selfish, and combative.

Content is critical, and mood, which is one dimension of content, is crucial. If the tone isn't right, you may as well hang up the phone. I'm talking about an easygoing mutuality based on shared interests, respect, trust, generosity, honesty, fair and consistent discipline, patience, humor, and expectation—a big order, but attainable even if imperfectly. Some families aren't *bad*; they just aren't "in sync."[1] Instead of parent and child engaging in an orchestrated dance, they are either out of step or dancing to different tunes.

My children and I were usually in sync. Within this atmosphere of mutuality all around, I enjoyed a special congeniality with Jennifer, our fourth. This doesn't mean that I loved her more and the others less; I value the four equally and feel closer to first one and then another, depending on the circumstances. Although comparisons are awkward, I want to relate my experience because it shows good and better ways of relating and testifies that fathers can change.

I was more comfortable with Jennifer, and she with me, because she came later in my life, when I was more knowledgeable, more experienced, and, of greatest importance, more mature as a person. With the older children, I was too demanding, especially of myself; as teacher, coach, critic, and keeper, it was my solemn duty to ensure that only good things happened. With Jennifer, I settled into an easier role. I was less often teacher and more often stimulator and clarifier. If I encouraged good questions, Jennifer could find good answers (or we could find them together). In *The Sense of Wonder*, Rachel Carson stresses authentic motivation: "Once the emotions have been aroused—a sense of the beautiful, the excitement of the new and the unknown, a feeling of sympathy, pity, admiration or love—then we wish for knowledge . . . It is more important to pave the way for a child to want to know than to put him on a diet of facts he is not ready to assimilate."[2]

In my more relaxed stance, I didn't pretend to know all the answers. If Jennifer asked why God allows snakes to eat baby frogs, I didn't pose as having a direct line into the Divine Mind; instead, the two of us explored the implications and drew some conclusions that served us well. Neither did I press her for instant answers. You've seen children who feel compelled to raise their hands even when they have nothing to contribute. Jennifer wasn't hooked on applause; she enjoyed learning and recognized it is a lifelong pursuit. With this attitude, she was philosophical beyond her years.

Since I less frequently put my authority on the line, it follows that I felt threatened less often.

Suffering fewer affronts, I didn't let my temper and hands fly as much. Jennifer didn't waste energy trying to decide how I was regarding her—she knew that I accepted her whether or not she turned in a superior performance.

Children need to experience success, but we cannot manufacture feelings of accomplishment; we can only facilitate them. We want our children to build happy, productive, moral lives, yet the most we can do for the young builder is to hold up some standards, help sort out plans and gather materials, and then back off and let him construct one wall and another, room after room. We can suggest options, open our own structure for inspection (but not encourage a replica), note serious flaws, bandage hurt thumbs, commend good work, and occasionally lend a helping hand. But we must not barge in and rip out features we don't like, or slip in and fix things to suit ourselves, or constantly show how to do things better.

If someone gathered us fathers for a pep talk and urged, "Jealously guard your child's self-esteem," many of us would nod agreement but then rush home and guard *our authority* even though we ourselves have suffered overbearing parents, teachers, and supervisors. I once had a boss who sat like a flexed steel trap waiting for someone to come along and nibble at his authority, whereupon he sprang upon the quarry in a rage. I was so intent upon avoiding his wrath I couldn't do my work. I have never had a good relationship with someone whom I feared.

It's strange that some fathers who embrace the human-potential movement are rigid parents. They have read the self-actualization books and taken the courses; at work and in their organizations, they encourage group process. But at home, they're tyrants.

A fetching concept in motivational theory is Douglas M. McGregor's Theory X and Theory Y.[3] I remember which is which because Theory X seems to "X-out" one's faith in people; it presumes that workers are naturally indolent and resistant, and you control them as you would a donkey: you either hold out the carrot or brandish the stick, because (it says here) the proper role of management is to direct, reward, and punish. Theory Y, in contrast, presumes that people are naturally motivated and cooperative. God made them that way. Management's function, then, is to enable the worker to do his or her own thing and do it well, for personal satisfaction and the good of the organization. Theory Y says, "I'm OK—you're OK."

Many fathers take a Theory X, or donkey view, of their children; they presume that the true nature of youngsters is to be perversely obstinate, and the most effective way to manage is to threaten or to buy off. I sometimes hear parents describe their children as they might hostile aliens from outer space—a different species. Embrace the Theory Y of child-rearing; assume that your children are basically good.

"I know a father whose word is law in his household," says humorist Richard Armour. "His wife and children tremble when he speaks. In fact he scares *me* a little. If I am too weak, he is too strong. I get love from my children, but not much respect. He gets respect but not much love."[4] I want to be flexible, but not so open-minded that my brains fall out. I want to be a *father*, not a pal. Fatherhood isn't something to be stretched this way and that like Silly Putty. It's refreshing to see a dad and child munching popcorn and giggling over television antics, but this same father must at other times inspire purpose and direction.

Professor Urie Bronfenbrenner, the Cornell psychologist, complains that when experts like himself urge, "Let your child be himself," parents interpret this to mean "Let your child grow up by himself." But children need to be *brought up* by somebody, Bronfenbrenner says. "It's important to them that there be someone on the other side of the seesaw, and that each reckons with the other."[5]

I stress congeniality here because it is harder to come by than the stricter discipline that will be discussed later. We are naturally serious-minded. How can we relax when we feel acutely responsible for our child's thoughts, words, and deeds? The answer is, we shouldn't feel so responsible that we are petrified at the thought of letting our child venture. We're good at saying "must," "ought," and "should." What we need to practice is: "Tell me how you feel about this" and "How do you propose to handle this problem?" and "Let's see if we can work this out together."

We must keep asking ourselves what we want our child to be and become. We want him or her to be an effective and decent human being—self-knowing, self-confident, self-actualizing, self-giving. This requires self-discovery, self-development, and self-discipline. Home must be a place where new ideas and new behavior can be practiced without fear of personal rejection or of recrimination.

Try this exercise. Imagine that you have been permanently cut off from your child and can no longer influence him. Reflect on your relationship. Ask yourself:

1. Which of my concerns were legitimate? Did I fret over things that didn't matter?

2. In what ways was I effective as a father? Least effective?

3. If I were doing it over, would I seek a different relationship? What changes in attitudes and behavior would I undertake?

Now return to your real-life situation. Ask yourself: What changes *will* I make?

"*If I were doing it over . . .* " Every seasoned father and many of the superannuated ones indulge this fantasy. C. William Chilman, writing in *Today's Health*, shares:

> I'd look at my wife more often—and with greater concern and compassion. I'd ask her how the battle went with her, and remember to *say* I loved her, not just assume she knew it. And I'd see the children, not as nettles and barbs to be dealt with, but as small humans with important needs and tender feelings. This sounds pious and oversimple, but I mean it. One can become . . . so absorbed with the control of children's disorder that living itself gets mislaid. I found myself overlooking the wonderfully funny details of the children's growing, missing out on the little ridiculous happenings I was too preoccupied to notice or not home enough to see. I kept forgetting we were people—a family of people.[6]

The message is clear and urgent: Be a "family of people" while you have the opportunity.

NOTES

[1] The term "sync" is used by Dr. David Massari of Philadelphia's Child Guidance Clinic.

[2] Rachel Carson, *The Sense of Wonder* (Harper & Row, 1956), p. 45.

[3] Outlined in *Management and Motivation*, eds. Victor H. Vroom and Edward L. Deci (Penguin, 1970), p. 306.

[4] Richard Armour, "Friendly Advice to New Fathers from an Old Pro," *Parents*, June 1967, p. 48.

[5] "Somebody—Let It, Please God, Be Somebody," *Time*, Dec. 28, 1970, p. 37.

[6] See Acknowledgments.

Faith,
Hope,
Love Abide

_____ **3**

I squirmed while our speaker painted his dismal picture. We live in an evil age in which parents are rendered ineffective by overpowering external forces, he said. Moreover, mothers and fathers are having to go it alone because nobody cares anymore. As he developed his thesis, I bristled. Parents need encouragement, not an invitation to surrender to social annihilation and feelings that God is dead.

In a discussion period, I acknowledged there are hazards. "But I don't want them to dominate my life-view," I said, "and neither do I want to invoke society as a scapegoat for my own failures—more families founder in the home harbor than on the high seas. If I despair of my world, I'll become ineffective and communicate futility to my children. Even if the past were as glorious as our speaker depicted it, we cannot go back and live in it, and neither can we hibernate awaiting a more enlightened day. If we are to live, we will live *now*—in our changing world with our contemporaries, who include many caring, helpful people.

"I consider this an exciting time to rear a family," I said. "Anyway, it's the only crack at parenthood that you and I will get."

An eloquent rebuttal, I told myself. Overstated, perhaps, but necessarily so to balance the speaker's own excesses.

My smugness was short-lived. When we adjourned for refreshments, a friend who was experiencing tensions in her own family marched up to me and, fighting tears, snapped, "Damn your optimism!" Then she walked away, leaving me stunned.

Whether or not I deserved her outburst, I could understand her dismay. How dared I be hopeful in the midst of chaos and despair? I don't mean to be glib, so let me declare right here that being a parent isn't easy.

As a society, we are frightened by wars, rumors of wars, and The Bomb. Crime robs us of security of our persons and property. In the midst of affluence, poverty remains a stark reality. We are intimidated by big government, big business, big labor, and big institutions. We are victimized by inflation, unemployment, the plight of the elderly, physical and emotional illness, and abuse of the environment.

The divorce rate has more than doubled in the last two decades; two of every five marriages dissolve, and the specter of breakup haunts intact marriages.[1] One household in six is headed by a single parent, and half the children born today will at some time live with only one parent.[2]

Item: *In Atlanta public housing, 91 percent of the households have only one parent present.*[3] **Item:** *Even Jewish families—which Christians have pointed to as*

A Father Shares

examples of stability—are coming unglued. A Jewish leader, deploring a divorce rate that has climbed from 6 percent to 30 percent in two decades,[4] *complains, "The Goldbergs are trying to keep up with the Joneses."*

Parents are absent from home pursuing careers, volunteer work, and amusements. In half of two-parent households, both father and mother work outside the home. Half of the mothers of school-age children are employed.[5] Many fathers are working overtime or holding two jobs. Transfers disrupt living patterns and separate the nuclear family from the extended family, depriving parents and children of guidance, support, and companionship. **Item:** *An Atlanta mother of three, now divorced, reports seventeen moves in twenty years, with seven changes of schools for each child. "Not much stability," she complains.*

Peer pressures, and enticements in the media, notably television, challenge parental influence. **Item:** *Each year, half a million teenagers run away from home.*[6]

Juvenile delinquency and crime are energized by cars, money, drugs, alcohol, guns, and protective anonymity. Almost half of all serious crimes are committed by juveniles. **Item:** *A fifteen-year old who shot a "dude" says, "Wasn't nothin'. I didn't think about it."*[7] . . . **Item:** *Three peeved youths sprayed gasoline through the change slot of a subway booth and set it afire, killing two women*[8]. . . . **Item:** *In a recent year, schools reported 204,000 aggravated assaults*[9]. . . . **Item:** *Half a million children under sixteen are involved in prostitution.*[10]

Manners and morals are in revolution, tilting toward materialism, hedonism, me-first-ism, and drug and alcohol dependency. **Item:** *Each year, more than one million teenagers become pregnant*[11]. . . . **Item:** *Teenage drinking, after rising steadily, has leveled off but involves younger kids.*[12]

Faith, Hope, Love Abide   **41**

Many parents and children feel driven, rootless, and restless. They redirect their anxiety and antagonism at each other and the community. **Item:** *Several hundred thousand children are abused annually.* [13]

Dependence on experts and the impersonality of supportive agencies impose upon parental authority. Dr. Kenneth Keniston, Mellon Professor of Human Development in the Massachusetts Institute of Technology, observes: "Once parents supervised the family's work, schooling, health care, and entertainment, but now they cannot possibly raise their children without outside help. They must rely on expensive and complicated technology and an array of often faceless professionals—a staggering surrender of control. There is no easy solution."[14]

Society can be uncaring. Dr. Bronfenbrenner, the Cornell psychologist, says that the disintegration of families isn't due to irresponsible parents or intractable children but to the indifference of the rest of society. The family receives low priority. We have to "create new conditions to enable families to do what they do better than anybody else," he says, mentioning changes in work patterns, neighborhoods, and institutions, and the establishment of good day care.[15]

I have devoted considerable space to this recitation of societal pressures and obstacles, and have sought to describe them forcefully because they are real and pertinent. I also stress them to counterbalance my own sanguine mood and outlook.

Without deflating these unfriendly pressures, I do want to let some air out of the notion that the "good old days" were an Eden for families, for such a perspective encourages us to hate our own age. Nostalgia has it that the agrarian era was peopled by robust families who zestfully and harmoniously worked, played, and worshiped together, sur-

A Father Shares

rounded by communities of grandfatherly and grandmotherly folk. Actually, for many children those yesteryears were oppressive and hazardous. They suffered physical and emotional disorders that today would be cured or controlled. Many never knew their mothers, who died in childbirth. Some children were worked cruelly and received only short and spotty educations. Hinterlands eulogized for pleasant socializing and self-entertainment often generated feelings of isolation, loneliness, and boredom.

The hippies didn't invent dropping out, and family estrangements aren't novel. In my childhood, kids ran away from home, and fathers (fewer mothers then) abandoned their families. Towns had their drunkards, infidels, ne'er-do-wells (some by virtue of inheritance), womanizers, prostitutes, racists, and murderers. Some kids got drunk, drove cars ninety miles an hour, taunted the constable, indulged in back-seat sex, and vandalized private and public property.

But enough. My point is, all generations are tested and feel they're hapless victims of fate. My quarrel with the speaker mentioned earlier wasn't on his cry of "Danger!" or his sympathy with besieged parents, but on his failure to espouse courage and hope. In fairy tales, villagers are repeatedly scorched by the dragon but do nothing except wring their hands and scan the horizon for the stout-hearted hero on his white charger. Today's real-life people, too, assume the posture of "victim" and suspend authentic living waiting for a modern-day knight to appear and slay their dragons.

If we are to live, we will live here and now. God has given us resources for facing up to the realities of the world. We must work out meaningful relationships and act responsibly—be existential! Although we will not act perfectly, we are nevertheless required to act, and act responsibly. This we can do. As Paul said, "I can do all things in him who strengthens me" (Phil. 4:13).

To begin with, couples who do not have children can ponder whether or not they want a family. There is a new deliberateness based on various factors, including these:

• Impact on finances, career, and lifestyle. Expenses rise, careers are curtailed. There will be a cramping of marital sharing, friendships, social activities, and coming and going. (Later, a burden of chauffeuring.)

• Fears that the marital relationship will founder.

• Concerns about world overpopulation, hunger, and disorder.

• "I don't think I would make a good parent" misgivings.

• Feeling "it's all right" not to have children regardless of your upbringing and your parents' desires—feelings encouraged by the woman's liberation and self-actualization movements. There have also been denigrations (sometimes overt, sometimes incidental) of motherhood and homemaking.

Statistics document the new caution. Although more Americans are marrying, the rate based on population has declined. We are marrying later and having fewer children (1.8 compared with 3.7 in 1957).[16] More divorced persons are not remarrying, and more than two million adults of opposite sex live together outside of marriage. (But these comprise only two percent of U.S. households.)[17]

"Should we have a baby?" Once the question was hardly an issue and was discussed in private. Now it is debated in seminars, books, and magazines, complete with fifty-question checklists to be worked on like a tax return. Celebrities announce their decisions via television talk shows: "I'm taking the summer off to have a baby."

Deliberateness is in order: reports of child abuse and neglect and juvenile delinquency are daily reminders that the decision to procreate is often taken too lightly. But in a perverse way, I'm glad Jo and I had our children before parenthood became a sticky issue. Having a family seemed a natural expression of our maturity and mutual investment. "Be fruitful and multiply" was our easiest commandment. But *four?* Although Jo and I didn't plan each pregnancy, we accepted it as a gift from God. Had we waited for a perfect time, we would have no children at all.

I find zero population growth easy to accept in principle, but not as an unbendable rule. Writer Otto Friedrich once asked: What if Joseph and Rose Kennedy, having given birth to Joe Jr. and Jack, had viewed all third children as a pollution of Spaceship Earth and called it quits?[18]

With the arrival of a child, equivocation should cease but sometimes doesn't. A friend, exasperated by his three sons and miffed at his wife over discipline, declared, "I've had it with you guys. From now on you can deal with your mother. Count me out!" Now, three years later, he has chosen to end his sabbatical. He wants back in, and he is encountering resistance. Parental contracts simply don't provide for three-year vacations.

* * *

In the early seventies, the media frequently shouted, "Can the American family be saved?" Typically, in 1973 we tuned in every Thursday to watch the latest installment in the disintegration of the real-life family of Bill and Pat Loud of Santa Barbara, California.[19] Meanwhile, thousands of our young roamed cities and countryside, many of them questing for values that they felt were missing at home.

Now, instead of bleakly printing the family's obituary with great consistency, the media are publishing favorable prognoses and inquiring what can be done to improve its health. Even the "hippie generation," who changed our lives so profoundly for good and bad, has been absorbed into the mainstream, where they fret over rearing their own young.

The brighter reports include one by Paul C. Glick, senior demographer of the Census Bureau. With perhaps a dab of fond rationalizing, he sees sunshine glinting through gloomy statistics: The high divorce rate (stable for two years and expected to change less in the 1980s than in the 1970s) suggests fewer spouses trapped in unhappy marriages. He says children of divorce may—following adjustment —also be better off. In delayed marriage, he sees a more rational choice of mates; in later parenthood, fewer unwanted births.[20]

A survey published in *Psychology Today* found that married people generally feel better about their lives than unmarried individuals. Although children increase stress and somewhat decrease satisfaction, parents nonetheless indicate a higher level of contentment than unmarried groups.[21]

In a Louis Harris survey conducted for Playboy Enterprises, men aged eighteen to fifty were asked to rank values that contribute to a life of satisfaction. In a reversal from traditional male opinion, they put family life above work.[22]

Of 80,000 women who responded to a *Redbook* questionnaire, 43 percent said their lives were going smoothly with few problems, and 37 percent checked "difficult but fulfilling." Overall, motherhood was ranked the most important event in a woman's life, and two-thirds said they would

A Father Shares

feel incomplete if they didn't have a baby. Only 6 percent did not want children. (The ideal is two, spaced two or three years apart.) Prospective mothers expected their baby to have a positive effect on their marriages, and mothers confirmed this result.[23]

Jane Howard, author of *Families*, says: "Families aren't dying. The trouble we take to arrange ourselves in some semblance or other of families is one of the most imperishable habits of the human race. What families are doing, in flamboyant and dumbfounding ways, is changing their size and their shape and their purpose." She predicts that tomorrow's couples will be more mature, more experienced, and better prepared for child-rearing, and the fathers will accept larger roles.[24]

Lois A. Lund, dean of the College of Human Ecology, Michigan State University, says the family will continue to prevail because it alone has the capacity to teach children their true worth. "We don't give parents enough credit for their role as the first educators, and, I would say, the foremost educators."[25]

And so the predictions have gone, varying with the times and the "expert." The family is so vital, it is no wonder so many observers venture to assess its health. Alas, something so objective defies accurate measurement. Some of the suggested family substitutes (for example, "group marriage," in which three or more persons live together conjugally) have about as much substance as goldfish-swallowing and phone-booth stuffing. Norman Lobsenz, a writer specializing in family matters, says, "A lot of statistics are untrustworthy, and statistics are being turned inside out. In this field, you can say almost anything you want, and it's just as true for some people as it's false for others."[26] In a similar vein, Columbia University sociologist

Amitai Elzioni acknowledges that "the record of social scientists in predicting social developments is very poor."[27] (Partly in jest, I suggest that for contradictory views on child-rearing one need only look at the letters columns of professional journals.)

I respect most of the experts having academic, "union-card" credentials, and I quote many of them in this book, but I do not stand in awe of them. For one thing, authorities, too, live (or have lived) in families, and their personal experiences contaminate their views just as my own color my writing. Moreover, specialists are problem-oriented and inclined to view with alarm. Workers in a children's hospital, surrounded by sick kids, tend to view the general pediatric population as ill.

In a *Psychology Today* review of *Families* (a book mentioned earlier), Benjamin DeMott, Amherst College professor of English, praises author Jane Howard for being responsive to fresh currents that others are obliged, by dogma or dread, to ignore. He says the culture-critic clan is enormously useful as chroniclers of loss and deprivation but is usually ridden with nostalgia. The members "behave as though current experiences of release, opening, and promise are somehow unreal," he observes, adding that where Howard's temperament is constructive, many commentators add to the problem.[28]

The authorities are so gloomy! Eda LeShan, herself an educator, family counselor, and author, perused thirty child-care books for a *New York Times Book Review* commentary and reported:

If I were a young parent today, I might cut my throat. There is little joy in most of the books; raising a child seems to have become about as pleasurable as trying to build a house without blueprints, and with faulty materials. . . . Instead of using the insights of science to help us develop the

A Father Shares

art of parenting, we seem to be trying to make parenting a science. In this attempt what we come up with is pseudoscience."[29]

I have my own bias about families. I am, as my distraught friend charged, an optimist. I have come to this position by way of contrasting paths: *joy* and *depression*. Through do-it-yourself therapy and family support, I have all but conquered the depressions (more reason for celebration), but I retain an acute awareness of how destructive pessimism can be. I acknowledge the obstacles but choose to emphasize our resources, including power and resiliency, for fulfilling our destiny.

We have friends whose two little boys have serious health problems. The older lad has diabetes.

"What care does he require?" someone asked the father.

"Diet control and insulin shots twice a day."

"Who gives these injections?"

"We do—my wife and I."

"How long has this gone on?"

"He was diagnosed at four and now he's seven—three years," the father replied.

"How often has someone else given him the shots?"

"Hmmm. Once. We were at the hospital with his brother."

"That's really amazing!"

"Not really. He has this need and we provide it. Quite gladly, I might add, because he's a joy in our lives."

My friend exhibits a responsible optimism which provides meaning and joy for himself and his family.

Anthropologist Lionel Tiger holds that optimism is biologically programmed into the human race. In *Optimism: The Biology of Hope,* he says the tendency to aspire and presume success has been a-building in our genes ever since our ancestors found the courage to attack those beasts whose likenesses grace cave walls.[30] I lack the sociobiological background to reckon knowledgeably with Professor Tiger's theory. But I *am* optimistic, and for my own reasons: Optimism feels good; it works; and it is my moral obligation. Pope John Paul I, in his last audience, held the day before he died, called a young boy to his side, and then he proceeded to share truths with the crowd. One of these verities was: "Hope is not a passing thought. Hope is an obligation of all mankind."[31]

For a third "great commandment," I nominate: "You shall be optimistic." In the thirteenth chapter of I Corinthians, we are reminded that our most earnest pursuits, like our fads and foibles, will pass away, but then we are given a promise of something that will endure. "Faith, hope, love abide. . . ."

NOTES

Recommended: Dr. Benjamin Spock, *Raising Children in a Difficult Time* (W. W. Norton, 1974; Pocket Books paperback).

[1] Bureau of the Census and National Center for Health Statistics.

[2] Bureau of the Census and Department of Labor.

[3] Atlanta Housing Authority.

[4] American Jewish Committee.

[5] "Real Kids vs. 'The Average' Family," *Psychology Today*, June 1978, p. 14.

[6] Office of Youth Development, Department of Health Education, and Welfare.

[7] "The Youth Crime Plague," *Time*, July 11, 1977, p. 18.

[8] "Token Clerk in Bulletproof Booth in Brooklyn Is Beaten and Robbed," *New York Times*, Feb. 25, 1979, sec. 1, p. 2.

[9] National Institute of Education.

A Father Shares

[10]Stephen F. Hutchinson, Odyssey Institute of New York.

[11]Planned Parenthood Federation of America.

[12]National Council on Alcoholism study by Morris E. Chafetz and Howard T. Blane, published in *Psychiatric Opinion*. Reported in *New York Times*, April 29, 1979, sec. 1, p. 19 and sec. 6, p. 45.

[13]National Center for the Prevention and Treatment of Child Abuse and Neglect, Denver.

[14]Keniston is the principal author of *All Our Children, the American Family Under Pressure* (Harcourt, Brace, Jovanovich, 1978).

[15]Urie Bronfenbrenner, interview with Susan Byrne, "Nobody Home: The Erosion of the American Family," *Psychology Today*, May 1977, p. 41. Adapted from *Who Cares for the Children?* an interview tape (Science Interface, 1977).

[16]Statistical Bulletin of the Metropolitan Life Insurance Co.

[17]Bureau of the Census.

[18]See Acknowledgments.

[19]" 'An American Family'," *Newsweek*, Jan. 15, 1973, p. 68.

[20]Susanna McBee, *Washington Post*, in *Atlanta Journal*, Feb. 15, 1979, p. 10A.

[21]*Psychology Today*, May 1975, p. 37.

[22]"Survey Shows Most Men Give Family Life Priority," *New York Times*, in *Atlanta Constitution*, Jan. 22, 1979, p. 3B.

[23]Claire Safran, "What 80,000 Women Can Tell You About Your Biggest Decision—Having a Baby," *Redbook*, May 1978, p. 120.

[24]Jane Howard, *Families* (Simon and Schuster, 1978), p. 13.

[25]Press association interview, 1979.

[26]Jon Nordheimer, "The Family in Transition: A Challenge from Within," *New York Times*, Nov. 17, 1978, p. 1.

[27]"The Family: Holding Its Own in a Period of Changing Values," *New York Times*, Aug. 5, 1973, p. 54.

[28]Benjamin DeMott, review of *Families* by Jane Howard, *Psychology Today*, July 1978, p. 108.

[29]Eda LeShan, "Child Care," *New York Times Book Review*, Feb. 20, 1977, p. 26.

[30]Lionel Tiger, *Optimism, the Biology of Hope* (Simon & Schuster, 1979).

[31]"John Paul Added Humor to His Papal Audiences," United Press International, in *Atlanta Constitution*, Oct. 3, 1978, p. 12.

A Father Shares

In the
Beginning...

4

My first date with Jo came out of a misadventure.
I took another girl to a district picnic of the Epworth
League, then the youth arm of the Methodist
church. While I was playing tennis, she went into
town with some boys, and when she didn't return, I
asked Jo if I could take her home. I'd been wanting
to date her. Her black hair cascaded over her shoulders and her soft, brown eyes bespoke both sensitivity and fun, causing me to wonder if she was as
shy as she appeared. And I'm sure her trim figure
had its appeal.

As we were leaving, my date drove up and I
invited her to get in. Jo innocently scooted over
against me. The other girl sat next to the door, and I
whisked her home, whereupon Jo and I continued
our journey—a journey we have not yet completed.

We dated through the summer. I went away to

the University of Alabama and Jo worked and attended business college. With the outbreak of World War II, she worked for the government, and I became an aviation cadet. I washed out and came home on furlough before shipping overseas. We married, had ten days together, then spent two years apart.

I returned from the Pacific to resume my honeymoon and my education. Everything was auspicious except for an opinion from Jo's doctor that she might never be able to get pregnant. Maybe he was wrong. Besides, we weren't in a hurry.

Two months later—morning sickness, another trip to the doctor, and word there would soon be three of us. I was overwhelmed. I had counted on being a father *some*day. Now that eventuality had crystalized into a date only seven months away. I worried about assuming a father's responsibilities (whatever they might be) and the impact on my studies, our finances, and our living quarters. But in time thoughts of how much I loved Jo and of the great mother she would be chased the gloom away and the prospect seemed attractive.

My twelve-hour wait in the hospital was frustrating. Although a partner in this venture, I was being excluded from its conclusion. Still, having been in the labor room, I preferred my role to Jo's. I would never again put her through this—but *if* she insisted on having another child, I would demand my share of Demerol.

The waiting ended, a new life began—and there was new life in our union. Out of our bodies and spirits, Jo and I each had contributed an essence of ourselves which, receiving God's nurture, had blossomed into a complete, healthy, beautiful, and cuddly little girl, Barbara Jo.

How magical these first moments. As I count fingers no larger than birthday candles, watch

A Father Shares

blood pulsing through tiny vessels, and marvel at the variety of her moods, it seems that God is looking over my shoulder.

"What do you think?" he whispers.

"I think we've done a great job."

"You, Jo, and me?"

"Yes, although I had little to do with it."

"Shush! Admit you're proud."

"Yes, proud. But also humble."

"That's good. Keep it that way, proud but humble."

Later miracles are never so breathtaking as the first you experience. Bugg's Law of Diminishing Exposures testifies to the extra attention that's paid the first child: "There will be twice as many photographs of the first child as the second—the second as the third—the third as the fourth."

With Barbara's arrival, a luxury camera became a necessity. No sooner had I laid hands on that Argus C-3 than I snapped off thirty-six pictures. Look inside this tattered album. She was seventeen days old. See how she kicks in protest of this bother?

Time passes. A smile redeems a prune-smudged face. Stained pants testify to a fondness for playing in mud. A doting little mother sits under a Christmas tree clutching a doll named Ruthie. And see these painfully dressed-up children? The one with the contrived grin is the Birthday Girl.

But on this next page, someone new. Soft, brown eyes shine from a full, happy face. This is Randy. You'd know he is Barbara's brother by the way she's hugging him.

There's such a continuity of relationships that I almost forget that in five years we had five homes. From Tuscaloosa, we moved to Dadeville, where I managed my father's weekly newspapers. Next, Atlanta, where I did graduate work at Emory University and worked for the *Journal*. Next stop was Birmingham, where I headed the journalism department of Birmingham-Southern College and worked on the *Post-Herald*. Finally, we returned to Atlanta and I worked for the *Constitution*. It was here that Larry was born. His antics will enliven these pages, but for now I want to hurry along and complete the cast.

When the birth of our fourth child was imminent, my mother came over from Alabama to help us, as she always did. We were gathered in the back yard and the chickens on the grill were turning golden when Jo informed me that the intervals between contractions had shrunk to six minutes and we ought to be on our way. She gave each child a hug and kiss and the obvious admonition, "Be good for grandmother." As the two of us drove away, we glimpsed Randy running from house to house announcing, "Mother's on her way to the hospital to have our baby!"

This time I affected the nonchalance I had envied in old-timers. As I flipped through magazines, I recalled how Barbara had begged her mother to have another child—a girl. She adored Randy and Larry but they couldn't satisfy her hunger for a baby sister. If we pointed to the additional cost and work, she declared, "I'll do *anything!*"

We all wanted a girl, but now I told myself and God that either gender would be fine. But if it *were* a boy, what would we call him? After Larry was born, we had a name left over—Jennifer, for the spunky, compassionate little heroine of Barbara's favorite books. Clinging to that name and hoping to round out our family at two boys, two girls, we'd neglected to choose a masculine name.

Jennifer it was. Her blue eyes and tawny hair were a surprise, for Jo and I have black hair and brown eyes and the first three children followed the pattern. Later they would tease, "Jennifer, you've ruined our family."

I felt very close to Jo as I watched her nurse Jennifer. "I have a special feeling," she said, "a sense of completeness. I don't know any other way to put it except 'My cup runneth over.'" She had captured my feelings perfectly.

* * *

From the beginning, we've been close. Each newcomer was welcomed by Jo and me and whichever older children were already on the scene. The surest way to live happily ever *after* is to live happily *before*. But it is in the beginning that fathers begin slipping. Here are some of the pitfalls:

Male stereotyping. From our blue-bootee days forward, we're conditioned to be tough, stay on top, swallow hurts, keep our own counsel; we're more comfortable talking about *doing* than *being*— about *things* rather than how things affect us. Strength and self-reliance are wonderful gifts, but overdone they keep fathers and children at arm's length. Without vulnerability, there can be no intimacy.

We don't believe fathers can "mother." I fed and changed our babies, washed them and their diapers, cuddled them on my shoulder and soothed fevered brows. But many new fathers have never held a baby. The writhing body and wobbly head cause them to feel uneasy.

When Barbara was ten days old, our doctor dropped by to check on us. Weary, he sprawled on the bed alongside Jo and lay contemplating me as I gingerly cared for the little one. "Hey, relax!" he advised. "She won't break." I did—and she didn't. After that, I felt comfortable.

I'm tempted to urge that you develop an easy manner with your baby "even if it kills you." While I was producing publications for a children's hospital, I became acquainted with a condition called rumination (the cud-chewing cow ruminates) in which infants chronically spit up. Observation may detect tension in a parent, usually the mother because of her primary role. Often unaware, the mother handles the baby uneasily or holds him at a distance as an expression of her anxiety, fear, hostility, or ambivalence. Rumination isn't widely discussed for fear mothers will blame themselves and tighten up even more. Therapy consists of helping the mother to understand the baby's ways and to appreciate her new role, plus practical tips on care. I don't want to encourage self-diagnosis; my purpose is to stress the infant's need for confident and loving handling from both parents.

If an uncomfortable father doesn't get the guidance that he needs at home, he might solicit professional help. Pediatricians and pediatric nurses are very good at enhancing parent-infant relationships, and a modest fee will be money well spent.

We disdain "baby" games. Define "game"? A man will stress competition, which is why he may regard as pointless Cough-and-Smile and Peekaboo. Actually, early participation in simple games facilitates the baby's development and satisfies many basic needs. I ridiculed Jo's reading aloud to six-word-vocabulary infants, but she was right—she was building rapport and starting a good habit. Fathers, too, can read, sing, tell stories, go for strolls, and call attention to interesting things.

We fail to go all the way. Dr. Matti Gershenfeld, Temple University psychologist, identifies four basic elements of parent-child interaction: touching, physical proximity, eye contact, and conversation.[1] Employ all four and you really score. If, for example, you sit on your child's bed, look into his face, say "I love you," and give him a kiss, you've scored in all four dimensions. If, instead, you merely call goodnight from your easy chair—one. And you've saved what? Three minutes?

We're breadwinners. Many men identify themselves first with their occupation and only then with their family. If you meet a man and ask him to tell something about himself, you don't expect him to blurt that he's a husband and father—poor fellow, he ought to say he's a plumber or a banker. But we think it normal for a woman in Phil Donahue's audience to introduce herself as a wife and mother, give the names of her children, and add that they're good-looking, well-mannered, and the joy of her life.

Why be a work animal when, instead, you can be a complete person?

We get a late start. For nine months, the baby is "in there," remote and inaccessible. And then there is often a separating glass wall. The harried father must visit the hospital, attend to phone calls, do errands, finish the nursery, and perhaps tend other children, meanwhile battling a backlog on the job. Not the ideal start.

Pediatrician T. Berry Brazelton observes that the mother-child bond is quickly cemented—it's *her* baby and dad is left out. He says that during the first eight weeks he himself had a rather remote interest in his own child." I felt estranged from my clucking, involved wife. But when a little later the infant began to smile back at me and respond openly, I was caught—as most young fathers are. From then on it was easy sailing as I became more and more involved with 'my' baby."[2]

Fathers are becoming more interested in and better informed about the progress of the pregnancy. They're helping to decide about doctor, hospital, delivery. They're taking preparedness courses, attending the delivery, and participating in the infant's care. One success breeds another.

We lack patience. *Baby* is a synonym for "cistern." And jaws that lock against feeding make you fear tetanus. With age, the youngster becomes more devious, more skilled. A three-year-old can run like a racehorse and ask all sorts of difficult questions like "Why?" and "Where is the doggie's mommy?"

Father, exasperated from flying solo, hands the child over to his wife unmindful that she too grows tired and irritable. We fathers should (1) allow ourselves to relish enjoyable activities; (2) be philosophical about chores that are tiring and boring; and (3) whether a task is difficult or easy, appreciate that we are making an important contribution.

We're jealous. I tolerated Jo's doting attention to tiny babies but later wanted to protest, "Hey, I was here first!" When I needed to be very close to Jo, children often got in the way. At first I couldn't accept the idea of a miraculous supply of love (as opposed to the "fixed economy of love" concept wherein somebody's gain is someone else's loss), and even when I did come to appreciate it, there was the problem of limited time. When Jo spent time with the children, there was less time for me, and occasionally I had difficulty accepting that. Moreover, sometimes I didn't express my needs openly.

Fathers should be generous and may at times need to be scolded child-fashion, "Wait your turn!" But our needs, too, are important. Fathers can initiate changes whereby there will be more time for adult conversation and intimate sharing. And sometimes wives are more receptive than we suppose, and our underestimation gets in the way.

* * *

We have these handicaps; however, they seem inconsequential compared with all that we have to share.

First, we can be partners (not helpers) in parenthood. Fathers are said to be special, but I fear "special" implies that their participation is valued because it's rare. Fathers can be special because they share with every opportunity, and even when they're absent, their spirit continues to inspire and comfort.

We can contribute to our child's physical, psychological, and spiritual growth and well-being. Out of our experience and insights, we can help our child to like himself; be appreciative of others; see order and beauty in life's patterns; cherish integrity; cultivate his faith; contribute to his world.

Second, we can utilize our gift of maleness. We can model the venturesome, resourceful, decision-making, family-protecting, God-venerating, patriotic male person—husband, father, friend, neighbor, and citizen, and meanwhile permit the child to peek through the visor of our armor and see a person who's also tender and vulnerable. In shared activities, including play, we can help our child to perceive himself complete and competent. The father's influence on his son is obvious, but he's equally important to his daughter. Just the way he looks at her, touches her, speaks to her, can assure her she's a valued person in her own right, fortunate to be who and what she happens to be. She also learns how to relate to the male contingent.

In summary, a father can help his son to be a boy and grow up to be a man; his daughter to be a girl and grow up to be a woman—in the richest sense. We have this potential and must exercise it now. Some parents complain that their teenager has turned into a monster suddenly, but such transformations are more often gradual and often involve parental failures and excesses. We need to obey a venerable precept for consistency: "Train up a child in the way he should go, and when he is old he will not depart from it" (Prov. 22:6).

Try this exercise. Jot down the qualities you want your child to develop. Review your list item by item. Wherever you can make a significant contribution, make a check mark. Chances are you will have marked practically every item.

Dr. Benjamin Spock observes:

> It is caring for the child that teaches the adult what she's like, what she needs, what she wants, what fun she is to be with, how to communicate, how to show love to her, how to win love from her. These lessons can't be learned through words, only by living them. . . . The way for a father to become companionable with his children is to participate fully in the care of his first baby from the day she comes home and keep on participating.

And it's all right to make mistakes, Spock says sympathetically. "If your baby doesn't fall off the bed at least once, you're probably too worried and fussy about him, and that is something that could ultimately hurt his character."[3]

Viewing Barbara that first time, I felt proud and humble—and *responsible*. Even new machinery comes complete with instructions and special tools, but a baby is accompanied by nothing, not even a stitch of clothing. Nothing comes with fatherhood, either, and dad feels naked. He isn't handed instant wisdom, and even if he's handed an authoritative book, he recognizes he can't apply it word by word. Yet, there's something inside that compels him to commit himself to seeing that his child has good care and ample love.

There is no other moment like the beginning. It's too bad that the glow cannot last. *But it can!*

NOTES

[1]Carol Saline, "How To Have Great Times with Your Children," *Redbook*, Oct. 1978, p. 125.

[2]See Acknowledgments.

[3]Benjamin Spock, "A Father's Companionship," *Redbook*, Oct. 1974, p. 24. Also, interview with Betty Flynn, *New York Times*, in *Atlanta Constitution*, April 30, 1974.

The Pictures
in Our Heads

_____ **5**

Like Billy, the merry-go-round barker in
Carousel, expectant fathers fantasize what their son
or daughter will be like. In a word, *exceptional!*

Daughter? She will trail her mother until dad
comes home. Then, in dainty pinafore and with
ringlets bouncing, she will run and leap into his
arms, giggling. She will be intelligent, polite, and
domestic.

Son will be handsome and athletic, obedient but
spirited, smart but not sissy. He'll call "Hi" as he
wallops the ball over the hedge, then invite his
applauding father to pitch for both sides. He'll grow
up and win a good job and an attractive wife.

The child really will be exceptional—an exception
to what the father expected. How the parent re-
sponds will affect how the child accepts himself.

Jo and I had visions of what our little girl would be

and do, and for three years Barbara obliged with ladylike behavior. Then we moved and set her down in a neighborhood of boys. Again, she adapted, this time to pictures in the boys' heads. She became proficient at riding imaginary horses and shooting bad guys (and good guys). The boys didn't call her cowgirl (this was before cow*persons*) or require her to ride side-saddle; indeed, they envied her abilities. One little fellow threw himself upon the ground and cried because she (a girl!) shinnied up a pole he couldn't conquer.

We indulged these tomboy activities, reassured by Barbara's readiness to lope in off the range and change into feminine clothes and by her love for dolls. Occasionally she hooked a lad into playing mother-and-daddy.

Throughout her childhood, I supported Barbara's inclinations. I joined her in play and she joined me at work (sometimes I took her on my reporting rounds) because I loved her and enjoyed her company. Now I'm aware of broader implications. Challenging but supportive fathers rear venturesome and successful daughters. Example: Congresswoman Chisholm. Her father told her, "Shirley, you can do whatever you want; you have it in you."[1]

Stories of fatherly support are related in *The Managerial Woman* by Margaret Hennig and Anne Jardim. All twenty-five candidates for the master of business administration degree at Harvard who were profiled in the book recalled closeness with their fathers. Their mothers, too, were supportive, but mostly in confirming them as girls. The fathers assured them they had both the right and the capabilities to be more and do more than was traditionally expected of girls. One student recalled:

> I was Daddy's special girl. . . . He taught me to skate when I was four and he used to show me off to all

A Father Shares

his friends who had sons older than me. "See," he would say, "you think she is just a girl, but watch her out-skate those boys of yours." I always enjoyed those sessions, and afterward we would go to a soda fountain and have hot cocoa and he would praise me and brag about me to the druggist or anyone else who would listen.[2]

I don't want to encourage the manufacture of unwilling tomboys or M.B.A.'s, extensions of father egos. A father should encourage his daughter's total development, including the feminine side. Some fathers fail miserably. A woman now in her sixties recalls:

"Mother would get me into a pretty frock and do my hair. I would sit on the porch waiting for daddy. I *so* wanted him to say I looked nice, but usually he didn't. Mother would nudge him, 'Herbert, doesn't Susan look pretty?' He'd shrug, 'Pretty is as pretty does.' I'd be crushed. I grew up thinking myself ugly. [She isn't.] If a boy complimented me, I suspected an ulterior motive. I didn't feel comfortable around males."

It is impossible to trace out threads in a person's fabric, but perhaps I contributed some strong strands to Barbara's personality. She'll tackle anything. Her first full-time job was in a recreation center in a tough part of town. She has been a sales manager and a kindergarten teacher. She is a Girl Scout leader and trainer of leaders, day camp director, Sunday school worker, crafts instructor. She's expert in outdoor activities. And she's a dedicated and competent wife, mother, homemaker.

My experiences with my boys showed me how unreasonable expectations can be. Randy was welcome in the land of cowpokes but preferred quieter activities. Even as a toddler, he was neat. He grew up needing no prodding about homework, piano practice, or chores. The perfect son, right? Yet, Jo and I fretted over Randy's reticence to mix it up in rough-and-tumble play. We voiced our concern to our pediatrician.

"Doesn't the world need sensitive people as much as it needs tough people?" he demanded. "Don't we need piano players as much as football players?"

This truth, devastatingly simple, caused us to see the wrongheadedness of our excessive concern, and we relaxed. We did encourage male-oriented activities. Randy enjoyed Gray-Y sports; he went to camp every summer; became an Eagle Scout; joined a college fraternity and participated in its athletic program. He loves to ski, won a T-shirt in the last Peachtree Road Race, and is a good handyman.

No sooner had we begun appreciating tranquility than we were struck by a tornado named Larry. This kid skipped crawling in favor of flying. In diapers, he climbed our built-in china cabinet just to see what was up there.

As I went about renovating our house, Larry was my shadow. If I stooped to inspect something, I found him on his tummy beside me. Flattered, I bought some scaled-down tools and taught him to use them. My irrepressible student removed plates from baseboard outlets and poked in his screwdriver to generate fireworks. If I confiscated his tools, he improvised.

Once after I couldn't get into his room because the doorknob had been removed and hidden, I went to the basement and constructed a large wooden box fitted with compartments to be opened with screwdriver, pliers, and wrench, and outfitted with his favorite appliances. I presented him the plaything and his very own key and admonished, "When you feel an urge to tinker, tinker with your magic box." The diversion worked for a while.

Burned into my memory are misadventures in-

spired by "I wonder what would happen if..."
Four-year-old Larry was playing with matches behind the living room couch and set the ruffled curtains afire. He ran to the kitchen and cried, "Mama, come quick! Something bad is happening!" Jo found a wall in flames. She evacuated the children (she found Larry under his bed), had a neighbor call the fire department, and hurried back home. She and a passer-by subdued the fire.

Larry was Play personified. His uniform was torn shirts, muddy pants, and scuffed-out shoes; his credentials were detention slips; his motivation was dares from buddies. He wasn't mean, impudent, or wantonly destructive; indeed, he was polite, loving, and forgiving. But he had a warped set of priorities: television, comic books, derring-do, horseplay and applause—and only then studies and chores. He could not bring himself to accept unpleasant realities—for example, he waited for the protective squeal of school bus brakes to produce crumpled detention slips for signing.

We carped, threatened, and took away privileges, and I used my belt. Promises, but no lasting improvement. By tenth grade, he had a frightening educational deficit. We would have despaired except for his redeeming personality and love for us, plus reassurances from some adults (teachers, a counselor, scoutmasters, church workers) who had faith in Larry and occasionally drew out his best. But their predictions that he would ultimately find himself and succeed were whispers drowned out by the shouts of his misadventures.

Then a cousin, a child-development expert, leveled with me: "You and Jo are good parents, and you have a remarkable family. But, you know, it's easy to love the lovely, and it's difficult to accept and support the child who is doing unlovely things. Barbara, Randy, and Jennifer get along well with people and meet challenges handily, but Larry has difficulty measuring up to their achievements and your expectations. Larry keeps bumping against uncompromising walls and with every defeat becomes less willing to risk again. He needs time. Back off. I don't mean abdicate, but be more supportive and lay off the heavy discipline. He will soon begin maturing and you'll see remarkable changes."

Her counsel stung, but I respected her judgment and knew she cared, so we followed her advice. Within a year, the maturational clock inside Larry began ringing and the promised transformation began.

Now Larry is married and the father of a wonderful little girl. He's a good husband and father, and he has kept plugging away at college while holding a variety of jobs and winning support from mentors.

Why did he bloom late? He seemed a happy, well adjusted little fellow. We entered him in school a year too early—when he was six, and in second grade he had a teacher who raged at her class. We rescued him by getting him into a more advanced group, but already he hated school. No doubt, we let him down at times. Also, as my cousin said, he was sandwiched between successful siblings. Who knows, perhaps late maturation was in his genes.

Today, as I marvel at Larry's ideas, ideals, and achievements, those desperate years seem like a bad dream. Our closeness is especially gratifying because we have traveled a rocky road together.

"It's a wonder you didn't turn bitter," I said recently.

"I never doubted you loved me," he responded.

Discussing other aspects of adolescence, I remarked, "Sooner or later, every youngster has to leave home."

"Not me," Larry demurred, "I *never* left home."

Self-esteem is vital yet elusive. It thrives on loving and secure relationships, stimulation and approval, and acceptance of the child as he is rather than the way we wish him to be.[3] And, I would emphasize—never give up!

* * *

Self-esteem sprouts early, can wither early. A baby smiles and receives a smile in return—or doesn't receive it. A child who pulls up in his crib and looks around as if to say, "Hey, look at what I've done all by myself," either receives approval or doesn't. James Atwater, in *Today's Health*, tells how he and his wife expected to mold their baby girl.

> Here was this infant, born of an eager father and a marvelous mother, whom we could shape and inspire as we saw fit. The initiative was all ours. I would avoid with her all the mistakes that our friends were so obviously making with their children. I was assuming, of course, that Beth would develop along any lines that we laid out for her. Why shouldn't she? What did she know?

> Very soon, of course, it turned out that she knew a great deal. . . . In one of the most profound shocks a parent can perceive, a tiny, lovable creature reveals the fling and flash of character. From that point on, you should be wise enough to know that you cannot mold the character and life of your child as though you were working with clay. Yet we trespass.[4]

We trespass because of those pictures in our heads. Dr. Murray Kappelman, associate professor of pediatrics, University of Maryland, says the glowing unpredictability of each child is "a supreme experience of wonder" that too many parents fail to enjoy. Writing in *Family Health*, he notes that anxious fathers and mothers sometimes mistake slow development to mean a sluggish mind and parental failure. "But most children who do not fit into the pattern are exercising their right to be individuals, announcing to the world in general and to their parents in particular that they are themselves. They are individuals in the process of formation, each marching to his own rhythm, and each usually reaching the finish line at about the same time."[5]

We trespass. We try to invade our child's mind and oil the escapement to facilitate scholarship and win the prizes. Selma Fraiberg, author of *The Magic Years*, says we are overly preoccupied with the learning of content to the neglect of the *affective* side of learning: "a child's emotional breadth and depth, a child's capacity to love, derived from the experience of love, obtained hour after hour, and not marred by repeated disappointments and losses."[6] Margaret Mead said we rob the child of "joy of living; acuteness of sight, hearing, and touch; sensitivity to people's feelings and thoughts; special responsiveness to nature; the capacity to draw upon oneself."

We trespass. We coerce our children into careers of our own choosing. A son becomes an attorney and joins his dad's prestigious firm—and is miserable. A mechanic's son forgoes technical school for a business education—and is miserable.

I like the attitude of the Rev. Norman Neaves, United Methodist pastor of the Church of the Servant, Oklahoma City. In a sermon, he related:

> Just recently, my little boy Todd has been announcing that he wants to be a minister when he grows up. "Just like you, Daddy," he says to me, and of course it makes me feel very proud. But you know, each time Todd has made that statement, I've said, "Todd, I'm glad you're thinking about that and I think you'd make a good minister. But you'd be

A Father Shares

good doing a lot of things, and you might want to change your mind many times before you're grown up." If Todd had understood what I was saying, I might also have added, "and hopefully you'll always be open to changing your mind *even after you're grown up!*"

It's not that I don't want Todd to be a minister, because certainly that would be a very confirming "stroke" in my own life. Nor is it that I don't think Todd would be a good minister, because he does have a lot of good "people instincts" that are necessary in the ministry. It's just that I don't want him to get so locked into a particular vocational objective that he begins to close his mind to other vocational objectives. And moreover, it's just that I don't want him to feel like he's rejecting his daddy if he feels like rejecting daddy's vocation, or that he's gaining his daddy's approval if he chooses his daddy's vocation. Todd is Todd; like all of us he's capable of doing many fine things with his life, and I covet for him the freedom to be who and where he wants in the particular way and style that he chooses.[7]

I've tried to allow my children this kind of freedom and flexibility, beginning with Barbara's early aspiration to be a Florence Nightingale and Randy's to be a garbage collector like the friendly men who visited our alley and created the delightful cacophony of clanging and banging. The four have displayed a nice balance between earnestness and dedication, on the one hand, and self-assertiveness and risking, on the other. During high school and college, all held a variety of jobs—good orientations to the world of work and helpful in identifying careers they *didn't* want. I've mentioned Barbara's several vocations. I suspect Randy once considered the ministry. I'm glad we never pressed him to declare such an intention, because in college he inclined toward a foreign service career, then (following military service) entered banking. He attended night classes, took an M.B.A. in finance, and works as an auditor for a public accounting firm.

Larry began as a porter in a department store, cleaning rest rooms, among other duties. After becoming major-appliances sales manager, he decided merchandising wasn't for him. He pursued studies looking to a succession of career specialties and is now a supervisor for a parcel service.

Jennifer took a degree in psychology and worked as a waitress to earn money for graduate studies, then decided to defer school in favor of a tour of Europe, which is now in progress.

* * *

We feel so responsible! We want our child to succeed where we failed, do more and have more, be spared the deprivations—be like us, or different. So we push, sometimes unsure toward what. We faulted the youth of the sixties for being too activist—of the seventies for being apathetic. Our values become skewed. When Barbara left college after three years, a friend of mine said, "How tragic for her to waste all that time and money." Waste? Surely the college experience is worth something beyond a piece of parchment. Barbara uses her education every day.

Back when Larry was indulging his love of heights, speed, noise, fire, and laughter, Jo begged of a friend and fellow mother, "What can a parent do?"

"Jo, sometimes there isn't much we *can* do but love 'em," the friend said.

How true! When Jo and I became exasperated, one of us would say, "There isn't much you can do but love 'em," and we would manage a smile.

Once while watching a high school parade with a friend, I inquired about the woman's daughter.

"Judy? Oh, she's back there somewhere. She disappoints me so! I prod her, but it does no good. I was a cheerleader, May queen, all those goodies, but Judy isn't interested. I've given up on her. Thank goodness her little brother promises to be a winner."

"Let me share a parable," I invited. "A man had two sons. The older was quiet, studious, and dependable; the younger was gregarious, daring and fun-loving. Between them, they had every quality the father could desire; yet, he wasn't satisfied, because neither conformed to the picture in his head. Given the chance, he would have refashioned them into "perfect" boys—identical twins.

My friend was grinning sheepishly.

"What do you think of that?" I challenged.

"The father was foolish."

"Yes," I acknowledged. "I was a silly father." And we laughed.

"But you want to do *something!*" she insisted.

"Sometimes there isn't much we *can* do but love them."

NOTES

For advice on enhancing self-esteem, read Stella Chase and Jane Whitbread. *Daughters: From Infancy to Independence* (Doubleday, 1978) and Joy Wilt, *Happily Ever After* (Word, 1977).

[1]"To Dad, With Love," collected by Lynn Minton, *Good Housekeeping,* July 1975, p. 86.

[2]See Acknowledgments.

[3]Stanley Coopersmith, *The Antecedents of Self-Esteem* (W. H. Freeman & Co., 1967). Also U.C.L.A. psychiatrist Dr. Charles W. Wahl, quoted by the Associated Press. Also, the Rev. John D. Verdery, headmaster of the Wooster School, Long Island, New York, in a magazine article.

Concepts of the Swiss psychologist and development authority, Jean Piaget, are found in: Sidney Weinheimer, "How To Teach Your Child To Think: A Conversation with Jean Piaget, the 'Giant of the Nursery,'" *Redbook*, March 1972, p. 96. Also, "Jean Piaget: Mapping the Growing Mind," *Time*, Dec. 12, 1969, p. 61. Also, Dorothy G. Singer and Tracy A. Revenson, *A Piaget Primer: How a Child Thinks* (New American Library 1978).

[4]See Acknowledgments.

[5]See Acknowledgments.

[6]Robert Coles, "Talk with Selma Fraiberg," *New York Times Book Review*, Dec. 11, 1977, p. 1. Also, Selma Fraiberg, *The Magic Years* (Scribner, 1959), p. 301.

[7]Norman Neaves, sermon, Sept. 7, 1975.

Camping:
Ticket
to Adventure

6

Jo had refused to go camping—ever. "What if somebody or some*thing* should come along? No, you can take the kids and traipse into the wild, green yonder, but count me out!"

Yet, here she was with Randy, Larry, and me in this dark and desolate campground. I hastily built a cheery fire, which brightened her spirits and assured her there were no creepy-crawly critters (within the illuminated circle, at least). Later, the arrival of friends Gene and Lib gave her spirits another boost—their presence considerably reduced the chances that a bear would choose *her*.

Following a late supper of pepper steak (Gene mistakenly dialed the can's large hole), it was time for the supreme test, turning in. To be precise, it was our boys who pre-empted the station wagon and turned *in;* Jo and I turned *out*. Bedded on the ground, Jo discovered a new, wonderful world, and she insisted upon staying awake to celebrate it. In a sky that was bigger than any she had ever imagined, clouds scudded across a harvest moon. A breeze accentuated the chill, and we snuggled together under a blanket. Dredging up things she had somehow failed to mention in sixteen years of marriage, she was still chattering when I dozed off.

In the morning when I awakened her and put a cup of coffee in her hand, she complained, "I didn't sleep very well."

"Why?"

"A star kept winking at me," she said slyly.

Count Jo in!

For our first outing with the full family, I borrowed a tent. Making two trips in a rented boat, I ferried the tent, a conglomeration of household goods, and our hardy band of pioneers across a lake to an island. Barbara and Randy served as an advance party and surprised us with campcraft garnered from youth-group experiences. They erected the tent on a pad of pine straw, dug a latrine, laid a fireplace, gathered wood, and sunned our bedding.

We were apprehensive over Jennifer, who was only two, but she took to camping as a duck takes to water; indeed, we all took to camping *and* the water. Fishing was bad but rock-skipping and bathing were good. We cooked hamburgers and potatoes on hot coals and ate them with a salad. Munching chocolate-covered grahams, we sat beside our fire and talked and sang.

At the children's bedtime, we went into the tent and I began telling them stories. Appropriate of nothing, Jennifer kept singing out, "Tee, hee, hee, you can't catch me on a Christmas tree," triggering uproarious laughter. I went outside and presented melodramas of shadow-figures formed by my hands and fingers, projected onto the tent wall by the firelight. Soon the four of them were asleep.

Jo and I huddled by the fire drinking coffee and listening to the lapping of the lake, the *chur-rump* of a bullfrog, and the *Who cooks for you? Who cooks for you-all?* of an owl. "Taps" floated over from a scout camp. Everyday concerns—the No. 6 bus, my job, the PTA, household bills—seemed a million miles away.

That summer, we camped under a piece of discarded tarpaulin. Next year, we managed to buy a tent—barely, for it was a nine-by-nine model. Eager to test our "regulation" shelter, we arrived in our chosen campground and spread the canopy on a sandy apron and then pounded in the stakes. I reached for the box containing the poles and center assembly. It was not there; it was back home in the garage. Jo whisked the children aside and shushed them. I stewed for a moment, then framed the top of the tent with four sticks and tied it out to nearby trees, and we proceeded to have a wonderful vacation.

Seasoned, we aspired to push back our horizon. We were fascinated by a *National Geographic* report on the Outer Banks of North Carolina, a chain of oversized sandbars that venture thirty miles into the Atlantic to flirt with the elements and then skitter back to the safety of the mainland. The Cape Hatteras National Seashore promised seventy miles of open beach on three of the barrier islands. It seemed a daring place; photographs in the magazine showed where, the previous year, the storm-roiled ocean had bitten Hatteras Island in two.

"Don't go!" advised friends who had been there. "Nothing but sun, sand, wind, and sea."

"Go!" said another family. You'll love it. Nothing but sun, sand, wind, and sea."

We went. It was dark when we arrived in the Oregon Inlet Campground. Next morning, we climbed the barrier dune and gazed upon the heaving ocean. Seven-year-old Larry scrambled down the sandy incline and skittered along the water's edge as if compelled to cover the whole Atlantic seaboard that day. Zigzagging when the ocean took swipes at him, he paused occasionally to pluck an appealing bauble from its creamy setting and then streaked away again like a puppy released from confinement. "Wow!" he cried, "Wow!" I shared his elation but also felt a tinge of sadness because many youngsters never have this opportunity. Larry might have missed it had we not discovered camping.

Our destination was Ocracoke Island, and although a nor'easter was moving in, we headed south. We rode a free ferry (now there's a serpentine bridge) over to Hatteras Island, where we huffed and puffed up the 265 steps of the lighthouse (since closed) and gazed out on the Graveyard of the Atlantic. Then we took another free ferry to Ocracoke.

When we pulled into the beach campground, the storm was blowing full force and we despaired of erecting our tent. We drove into the village and took a motel room barely larger than our tent, and for two days the kids were like fish out of water. Worse, a third night's lodging at ten dollars would deplete our treasury and force us to head home. Next morning, I awoke to dazzling sunshine. "Everybody up!" I shouted. "We're moving to the beach."

During the next five days, we built sand castles, rode waves, caught all the fish and crabs we could eat, collected six bags of shells (after enforced culling), viewed the wild ponies, searched out wrecked ships, and explored the marshes. Noondays, we strolled the oak-shaded lanes of the village and got acquainted with the sturdy islanders and their Elizabethan "toime 'n' toide" speech. Evenings, we and fellow campers sat atop the dune and

A Father Shares

viewed the sunset, then moved down onto the beach to build a fire, toast marshmallows, chat, and sing oldies along with the youngsters' favorites.

When we departed Ocracoke, Larry declared we'd had "the funnest time of our lives." Everyone agreed, and every year since that first visit in 1962, all or some of us have returned to our magic island. No other place except home, church, and school has contributed so much to our lives.

In two decades we have camped in Maine, the Ozarks, the desert in New Mexico, and on Florida shores. The economy of sleeping in tent or trailer and eating off picnic tables has enabled us to travel twice as far and to stay twice as long as we could have done taking the creature-comforts route. As a bonus we have enjoyed wholesome outdoor living, closeness to nature, proximity to recreational facilities, flexibility of itinerary, and acquaintance with wonderful people. We have developed skills and resourcefulness, and we have drawn closer as a family while sharing chores and fun.

I recommend that you try family camping. Even the kid who has "everything" is poorer for never having lived out of doors with his/her dad. Camps for children and youth have their special values but cannot take the place of adventuring with one's family. Here are some suggestions:

For that first outing. You may want to rent or borrow basic equipment, which you can pre-test in your yard. You can gain training and enjoy security by going out with an established camping group sponsored by a church (described in chapter 9), youth organization, or county or municipal recreation department. Some provide basic equipment. Many novices thrive on their own, opening cartons of newly purchased equipment on their first outing. A good guidebook helps.

Buy equipment gradually. Good equipment,

carefully selected and properly maintained, will last five or ten years or longer and is economical when amortized over such a period. We began with our tarp. (Lacking privacy, it was better suited to yesteryear's less crowded campgrounds.) Then our tent. On the eve of a three-week journey into New England, we borrowed money and bought a tent-trailer. This wheeled box followed our station wagon so obediently that we had to remind ourselves it was back there; and in camp the canopy popped up presenting a boudoir furnished with two double beds plus floor space for two sleeping bags. A decade of hard use and Ocracoke storms ravaged the trailer. Now Jo and I are using a hand-me-down tent given us by Barbara and Harold, who have moved up to the trailer set.

For auxiliary equipment, we drew upon household goods—quilts, pots and pans, picnic ice chest. Gradually (mostly at Christmas and on birthdays), we added gear: gasoline stove, lantern, sleeping bags, air mattresses, plastic kitchen fly, cook kit, folding table, collapsible oven and dutch oven, homemade chuck box, and screened room. Somebody teased Jo, "You take more stuff camping than I've assembled in twenty years of housekeeping." And I added, "Yeah, we are going to roll into a campground followed by a van, and the driver will get out and inquire, 'Ma'am, where do you want the piano?'"

Be selective about campgrounds. Campgrounds vary. Some are delightful; others are eroded, littered, overcrowded, and poorly managed. Some draw joy-riders from nearby towns, members of the drug set, blaring tape players, barking dogs, and mosquitoes and flies. You can get a line on a campground from a guidebook, but it is reassuring to talk with people who have recently been there.

A camp*site* is an individual space within a campground, basically affording a place (some-

A Father Shares

times an improved apron) for tent or wheeled quarters; a picnic table; and a garbage can. As a rule, there will be a water tap; a fireplace or grill (sometimes shared); and flush toilets, centrally located. Most have showers (hot or cold), and some have sewer hookups for trailers. Most families prefer amenities and like to have neighbors fairly close by.

There are both government-operated (U.S. Forest Service, National Park Service, state, county, and municipal) campgrounds and proprietary campgrounds, with good and bad facilities within either grouping. Overnight fees begin at a couple of dollars in a public facility and run as high as ten for a specially located private site.

Plan your trip. In advance, check a directory. Some campgrounds offer reservations. Call ahead to check on availability, and it doesn't hurt to ask that a site be held for you. Arrive by late afternoon, earlier if you expect crowding. Have an alternate plan, especially important now that gasoline is expensive and less dependably available.

Consider the whole family. After I had described the delights of camping to a church group, a scowling woman marched up and complained: "Let me tell *you* about camping! Mama (that's me) is trying to keep the baby out of a yellow-jacket nest and the toddler out of the lake. Meanwhile, I'm hauling water, washing dishes, doing laundry, and splashing lotion on the kids' poison-ivy rashes. Daddy? Oh, he's out there on the lake with Junior. They'll be back for supper—except there won't be any, because we're out of fuel. Do you have the gall to call that miserable experience a *vacation?*"

I acknowledged that some families are callous or lazy. "Families who won't pitch in ought to eat out," I said.

Enjoy varied experiences. I'll discuss some possibilities in the next chapter.

How We
Discovered
America

7

Our vacations took on a new dimension when a Florida family inspired us to go out and discover America. We met them in a campground near Atlanta. A daughter would take American history in the fall, and the family planned to travel as far as Boston visiting scenes she would be studying. In Atlanta, they toured Civil War landmarks by day and then relaxed at their lakeside campsite.

To know a country, Thomas Jefferson wrote his friend Lafayette, "you must ferret the people out of their hovels as I have done, look into their kettles, eat their bread, loll on their beds." Taking that advice, we have craned at America's mountains, bobbed in her surf, hiked her deserts, toured her cities, visited her farms, met her people, and absorbed her history. The family proved to be ideal company for discovering one's roots, and our camp-

A Father Shares

ing mode tied us to the land and lent a "you are there" ambience. Indeed, our Studebaker Lark wagon, with people and cargo stuffed inside and gear lashed on top, resembled a Conestoga wagon.

Visited at the scenes of their exploits, history-book characters magically took on flesh. We sensed the genius of Jefferson, the courage of Washington, the passion of Patrick Henry, the perseverance of the Wright Brothers. Near Jamestown, we snuggled in our sleeping bags and imagined the anxiousness of the 105 men and boys who in May, 1607, bedded down on this soil. Next morning, as we tramped in woods, we fantasized meeting Captain John Smith and Chief Powhatan and Princess Pocahontas. Departing, we took a ferry across the James River. We looked back upon the moored replicas of the *Susan Constant, Godspeed,* and *Discovery* and conjectured how the shore might have appeared to the settlers when they arrived. Starved remnants of the colony attempted to flee this same shore only to have their rescue ship forced back. My teachers hadn't shared this unglorious evidence of human frailty.

Our favorite patriot is Jefferson, whom we met at Williamsburg. In the capitol there, we heard him debate English rule; in Raleigh's Tavern, we glimpsed him and other burgesses plotting against the royal governor; and in the Governor's Palace, we peeked over his shoulder and read General Washington's urgent appeals for supplies. Touring the countryside, we picnicked beside the Rivanna River, which Jefferson as a youthful canoeist proved navigable to the James, opening new markets for his community's produce. In Richmond, we toured the capitol, which he designed; and in the nation's capital, we studied his likeness in paintings and statuary, and we read aloud some of his vibrant prose. In the White House, we were reminded that President Kennedy told an assemblage of artists and scientists they represented the most extraordinary talent to gather there since Jefferson dined alone.

At Monticello, Jefferson's home near Charlottesville, Virginia, we were dazzled by the creativity of this man who at age thirty-two had won a reputation for being able to "plot an eclipse, survey a field, plan an edifice, break a horse, play the violin and dance the minuet." We halfway expected our redheaded host to amble into the foyer and check his seven-day clock, whose weights he accommodated by cutting a hole in the floor. We were awed by his patriotism. Through sheer determination, we were told, he staved off death until July 4, 1826, the fiftieth anniversary of the Declaration of Independence. Some of the patriotism of our national heroes rubbed off on us. We bought ourselves a flag, which we proudly fly at our front door.

History isn't sterile; it is brimming with emotion. One summer we were seeing our third outdoor drama of the season. During intermission, Jennifer, a precocious six, stretched and loudly asked her mother: "Which do you think is the saddest—'The Common Glory,' 'The Lost Colony,' or 'Unto These Hills'?"

We found connectedness in the sweep of history. At Williamsburg Gaol, the children locked one another in the stocks and pillory, and then as we toured the dank dungeon our guide mentioned that fifteen of Blackbeard's men had been incarcerated there. "Blackbeard!" Larry exclaimed. "We know all about him." On Ocracoke, we had fished in the outlaw's lair, a cove called Teach's Hole, and ashore the children had hunted for pirate gold.

"Colonial justice was very harsh," I observed.

"Yeah," Larry said, "but those pirates deserved it!"

A Father Shares

"What can I do for my child?" today's be-leaguered parent begs. Well, in Hannibal, Missouri, you can read aloud to him from *Tom Sawyer* while watching riverboats ply the Mississippi, then visit the young hero's cave and paint his famous fence. On the Old West Trail, visit Indian reservations and witness powwows and ceremonial dances, and intermittently explore the haunts of cowboys, marshals, and the black-hat set. In eastern Pennsylvania, poke along behind an Amish buggy while you munch hot pretzels and admire the manicured farms. Trace Davy Crockett to the Alamo; admire Misty's cousins on Chincoteague Island; look for Johnny Appleseed's trees in Indiana and Paul Bunyan's ox, Babe, in the North Woods.

If you're concerned about the erosion of values and morals, you will find shrines where discussions of fidelity and uprightness spring naturally. Meanwhile, your child will learn excellent ways to use leisure time and will develop an appreciation for the environment, and the whole family will enjoy refreshment and relaxation. There are reasons aplenty for going out to discover America.

Whatever your vacation mode, here are suggestions that will help you to enhance these shared times.

Evaluate your current patterns. Every major segment of our lives deserves a check-up now and then. In these days of inflation, are we getting full value? How can we conserve gasoline and other national resources without forfeiting pleasure? Our families change; have we made commensurate changes in our vacations?

Emphasize freedom of spirit. "Vacation" has a Latin root meaning freedom. It embraces both *suspension* of work or study and *diversion* into rest and recreation. But some families' vacations aren't freeing or relaxing; they are hurried and regimented and filled with the same hassles and boredom that spoil life back home.

We have practically made "vacation" synonymous with "trip," although a change of place may be less important than a change of pace and role. A holiday isn't the best time to lecture petty faults (it ain't a good time to combat "ain't") or "straighten out" someone. Planning and order shouldn't choke out spontaneity.

Visit nearby attractions. We are overdependent on the automobile. I'm not recommending asceticism but honest appraisal. As I have related, the automobile has enormously enriched our family life, but I don't consider our trip to Maine any *better* than vacations spent in our own north Georgia mountains—only *different.*

Every summer Americans play fruit-basket-turnover, and each arriving contingent oohs and ahs over things the departed residents have ignored. As an exercise, I quickly jotted down forty attractions within an easy day's drive. Half of them I have never visited. While neglecting these nearby attractions, my vacations have taken me into twenty-six states. We can catch up at home, yet enjoy variety. Most Americans can find strikingly different geography within two hundred miles.

Still, I must acknowledge that the only strictly stay-at-home vacation we have tried was flawed. We planned to discover our own city, swim, picnic, eat out, see movies, and be lazy. But as we unloaded groceries bought for the duration, our station wagon rolled down the driveway and plunged over an embankment, suffering a hundred dollars' damages. (I recovered the fifty-dollar insurance deduction by selling a piece called "Don't Say 'Stay Home' to Me.") When, at the end of the week, we got the car from the shop, we headed for the hills.

Some people can relax anywhere. Me—even wearing blinders, I would see grass that needs mowing, gutters that need painting. Another vacation at home? Perhaps, but I would spend a few days of it out of range of telephone, postman, and big and little neighbors.

Stay awhile. My father and brother drove from Alabama to New York City. They recruited a guide off the street and during a two-hour tour glimpsed several recognizable landmarks but failed to resolve which island it was that Peter-somebody bought from the Indians for twenty-four dollars, whereupon they drove directly home. Jimmy suggested stopping at Mammoth Cave, but dad demurred: "If you've seen one cave, you've seen them all."

Although whirlwind trips were better suited to forty-cent gasoline, they will persist. One youngster said of his father: "Once he gets under the wheel, he won't stop for even you-know-what." In my opinion, "Look at that!"-"Where?"-"Back yonder" trips are costly, unsafe, and cramping. They transform cooped-up children into guerrillas (or gorillas). And you get a blurred view of everything but gas pumps.

Several times, writing assignments forced us to tarry in locations where we would otherwise have passed through. Locales included the Elephant Butte desert lands in New Mexico; the Shepherd of the Hills country of the Missouri Ozarks; and Lake Winnepesaukee, a glacier-formed reservoir in New Hampshire. We got the feel of these regions and enjoyed our sojourns. In contrast, some people's vacations are mere samplers; they collect places to visit at greater length "someday."

Go home again. Although they likely would resist the suggestion, your children might enjoy family reunions, conversations with the elders, and visits to homeplaces. In Alabama, our four are awash in nostalgia. Here's the store where Grandfather Smith worked and treated them to pop and cigar boxes. In this oak-shaded yard, they played with cousins. Here, where my father cultivated his showplace garden, they remember gathering vegetables and sucking nectar from his scuppernong grapes. Mr. Parkman kept Bill, his "cow," in this pasture. Here's the street that led to town and ice-cream cones. Standing under the pecan trees, they swap stories of the outlandish things their grandmother did to entertain them.

Take advantage of the setting. In Pennsylvania, we ate shoo-fly pie; in Maine, fried clams; in Williamsburg, rock candy; in New Mexico, enchilladas. We gathered fruit from orchards, watched the milking of cows, observed boats going through locks, stood beside whirring hydroelectric generators.

Seize brief opportunities. Finding ourselves at Lexington with only two hours available for a trip into Boston, we decided to give it a whirl. We parked our trailer under the watchful eye of the Minute Man, drove into the city, and managed to tour most of the Freedom Trail.

Do some homework. In advance, get acquainted with the places you'll visit. Obtain folders from chambers of commerce, government agencies, museums, historical societies, travel agents, motor clubs, and transportation lines. Consult guidebooks, histories, and folklore anthologies, and talk with knowledgeable friends. Be aware that some attractions have limited seasons and close at a surprisingly early hour.

Seek ways to economize. Even when we aren't camping, we take along an ice chest and picnic basket and sometimes an electric percolator and skillet. Often we have breakfast in our motel room or at our campsite. Lunch is invariably something easy and light. Supper is a hot balanced meal. We pack our own break-time snacks. We've generally found the free or inexpensive attractions in a locale to be superior to ballyhooed satellite operations. We are easily entertained at small cost.

Guard against faulty expectations. They're the chief reason why vacations either explode or collapse. Some families expect too much, and are disappointed; some expect too little, and fulfill this outlook; and some entertain divergent and conflicting expectations. Solicit everyone's ideas in the planning. A vacation should afford each member some respite from routines. If you travel as part of your job, you may not be keen on a lot of eating out; however, your homebound wife may love it—and you might compromise. It seems to me that fathers most often dominate choices: "I earned the time off and I foot the bills." Or they abdicate decision-making but later second-guess.

Once itinerary and activities are firmed up, review them so that differences can be aired and accommodations be made. A "maybe" incubates in the back seat to become "But you promised!" and a mild objection grows into "I told you so!"

Who goes, who stays? When there were six of us, we rarely took a guest. We were already crowded; besides, we wanted our family to share without intrusion. When, later, there was only Jennifer, we often allowed her a companion. When children in their late teens had conflicting interests and schedules, we sometimes arranged for them to stay home. Ever make a trip with a recalcitrant teen?

Strengthen your spiritual life. Just as the Israelites religiously transported the ark of the covenant with them, so can modern families carry the essence of their faith along on their travels. Visit historic churches; worship with local congregations; attend services at resorts; have your own graces and devotionals; share with one another informally.

Seek adventure. Adventure depends more on boldness of attitude than of action. Allow yourself to be astonished by fresh experiences. Discover! Celebrate! Dream!

Walk a trail, rent a boat, ride a ferry, join a nature hike, prospect for minerals, catch some fish and cook them. We'll always remember the night when we first thrilled to the primeval, gurgling cry of a loon. The hearty goodness of our first dutch-oven cherry cobbler. Larry's nine-pound largemouth bass. The attitudes and skills we've gained continue to serve us well wherever we may be.

Aspire for quality. Vacation is merely a medium through which we make investments and draw dividends, usually in keeping with our effort and care. Some families bring home only burnt shoulders, frayed tempers, and strained finances. A proper vacation will be relished and cherished.

I'm glad I wasn't too immersed in my work to break away. I'm glad we didn't let budget limitations keep us at home. We went out to discover America; in the process, we discovered ourselves.

The Nature Club
Never Met

8

"Jo, I have an idea. Let's form a nature club—the six of us. We can make observations individually and then come together and share our findings."

"Umm, it doesn't sound like much fun."

Undaunted, I solicited Barbara and Randy. "Mom told us your idea," Randy said.

"Well—?"

"Please excuse us, dad," Barbara said. "We have to run."

The nature club never met, and I'm glad. It really wouldn't have been much fun and might have discouraged our spontaneous discoveries. In effect, we had a nature club all those years—our activities just didn't conform to my organizational-mindedness.

Larry, Jennifer, and I noticed cardinals plucking leaves off an oak tree and fluttering to the ground.

Were they eating the leaves? (Didn't seem tasty.) Building a nest? (Cardinals don't nest on the ground.) On inspection, we discovered blisters that I recognized to be galls, and when we pressed our fingernails into the bumps, we uncovered grub-like larvae. The cardinals were having breakfast.

A magnifying glass afforded us a better look and provoked more questions. Why had the galls formed? Was the leaf quarantining the invading insects? The encyclopedia had some answers but also said there are many things about galls that puzzle scientists.

The children's interest flagged and they ran off to join friends. We had enjoyed a delightful half-hour. How different it would have been if, at breakfast, I had announced, "Today we will study galls."

In our back yard and on camping trips, we observed myriad forms of wildlife. We also had many pets, common and exotic. I didn't realize how many until Randy looked up from writing and said, "We've had a hundred and twenty-six."

"One hundred and twenty-six what? I thought you were doing homework."

"I am. A theme on pets. Listen to my list: nineteen dogs, ten cats, one monkey, two possums, two ducks, one chicken, three snakes, seven turtles, two parakeets, three rabbits, two hamsters, six gerbils, three chipmunks rescued from cats, one squirrel, plus forty fish and twenty frogs and lizards—a guess, of course."

"Wow," I said. "That's a lot of livestock for somebody living only three miles from downtown."

"I'm glad you're finally admitting it," Jo grumped.

"Look," I remonstrated, "it isn't some kind of plot! These things just happen."

Like the night Barbara called me at the office and reported a strange creature on the back porch. "He's sort of like an overgrown rat." The other three clamored to share their own (and different) descriptions.

I got off early and, arriving home, recognized our visitor to be a baby opossum. For millions of years, these marsupials have resisted evolution, even clinging to their notorious ugliness. An explorer painted this quaint but accurate portrait: "Emonge these trees is fownde that monstrous beaste with a snowte lyke a foxe, a tayle lyke a marmasette, ears lyke a batte, handes lyke a man, and feete lyke an ape, bearing her whelpes abowte with her in an outward bellye much lyke unto a great bagge or purse."

But what did my children say?

"Isn't he cute?"

"He's darling!"

"He's neat. Can we keep him?"

"He wouldn't be much trouble."

I glanced at our vice-president in charge of muss and fuss. "Let's—"

"*Let's talk about it!*" Jo said, finishing my sentence. How often she had been outmaneuvered by this tactic. Whenever the children said of some appealing creature, "Can we keep it?" my response of "Let's talk about it" wasn't a promise of discussion but the subterfuge of an animal-loving father. This time we compromised: we would keep Little Possum three days to exhibit him at Jennifer's birthday party.

As the children said, he was no trouble. He spent his days sleeping, his nights clambering over the back porch, securing his perches with his hairless, muscular tail. He ate anything and everything.

The morning of Jennifer's party, five of us went

away on an errand, leaving Larry playing with friends. When we returned, he was in the kitchen crying. "Little Possum got away!"

"Where?"

"Under there." He pointed underneath a built-in bench. He had let a friend hold the possum and it had wriggled loose and scurried under the bench and up into the wall.

"What if he dies in there?" Jo moaned.

"We'll tear into the wall," I said. "But I think he'll survive—if you'd prefer a live-in marsupial."

Little Possum missed Jennifer's party but that night had one of his own. He consumed food and water left out for him, used the cat's litter box, and retreated to his lair. The next night we heard him clattering about and captured him. We released him in the back yard.

The following night, we answered the door and found a neighbor holding a cardboard box. "We heard your possum got away. We found this one and want you to have it."

I peered in at a whitish-gray puff. It glared back at me with beady eyes and a familiar grin. "Welcome home," I said.

The arrival of our most celebrated pet was announced by outraged jays and squirrels. High in an oak, a strange little creature was gleefully ripping nests apart. He was a squirrel monkey, the encyclopedia told us.

For weeks, the monkey entertained our neighborhood with daring acts, but then a chill in the air cautioned that he would have to be protected from the winter. We gained his confidence with food, then set our trap, an upside-down washtub propped on a stick to which we tied a string. When the simian ate his way under the tub, we yanked the string and collapsed the tub. We transferred the howling captive into a hardware-cloth cage equipped with several perches.

The children were ecstatic. "Bosco saved us fifty dollars," Jennifer glowed to friends. "That's what a squirrel monkey costs, you know."

Bosco was, indeed, appealing as he gazed at us from his off-white mask. He curled his incredibly long tail about his neck as a lady wears a fur. His orange forearms flashed as he grabbed grapes and bananas with his quick, black hands. He'd climb up and sit on our shoulders, but if we grasped him, he retaliated with shrieks and bites. We'd had Bosco a month when he developed sniffles. We took him to our vet, but he died of pneumonia.

Our Siamese cat, Philomenia, likewise "appeared." Extravagant rewards offered in the classifieds tempted the kids to open a truant-cat recovery service. Alas, the advertised cats were the wrong colors or sex (an inappropriate word in Philly's case). This cat was its own reward. "Think," Larry exuded, "a gen-u-wine Siamese for free!" The "free" bit was a cruel joke. After we insisted that Philly take a pre-bedtime stroll as our brindle cats had done, she developed sinusitis and a twenty-two-dollar vet bill.

The name Philomenia did not pop magically into our heads. You can call a mixed-breed just anything, but for a Siamese, "Kitty Boo" won't do. While we were racking our brains for a regal name like Ming Dynasty Third, only friendlier, Jennifer came home from next door with "Philomenia." Too late, our neighbor informed us that what she had in mind was Philomela, for the princess who turned into a nightingale.

Philly's palate attested to her royalty. She condescended to eat the more expensive cat foods only if we added affection and broth of guinea hen. Eat from the table? She did precisely that whenever our cuisine tempted her.

Philly slept with Jennifer—unless we had guests. On these occasions, we would hear footfalls, a plop in the hallway, the closing of a door and a demonic cry which Siamese fanciers say is "unlike any other breed of cat." I say unlike any other breed of *anything.* I would get out of bed to be startled anew by the gleaming sapphires in the wedge-shaped face. I would tote Philly downstairs, where she would lick at proffered cat foods, then hop back upstairs and snuggle against Jennifer until daylight, when she would sound an alarm that made a rooster's crowing seem a whisper: *Ber-r-r-ger-r-r-row!*

We had a rule against the Easter feathered set but relented and accepted two ducklings when friends who had tired of them said "or else—" Children love cuddly duckies, and Larry, three, loved one to death. He handed the limp-necked victim to Jo. "Put him to bed, Mommie, he's asleep." Jo found all available replacements wrong in size, color, and voice. Fortunately, a near-look-alike was never suspected to be an impostor.

Little ducks grow into big ducks. I can see Barbara clambering out of the basement mornings with a noisy fowl under each arm taking them to their pen. They began attacking Jennifer and we sold them to a poultry dealer who mentioned having a farm pond. Four dollars in hand, the children wanted to reinvest, but we had spent twice that much on food pellets.

On a picnic, Larry called from a stream, "Mama, I've caught a snake!" He ran up and thrust the small (*small?*) reptile in her face, whereupon she spilled hamburgers off the grill. A jar would be a more appropriate place, I suggested. Traveling home that night, there was a telltale metallic plop. Barbara was out of the car before it stopped. Larry and I got the

A Father Shares

snake back into the jar, but Barbara and Jo wouldn't get back into the car until we locked the jar inside the glove compartment.

Our less notorious pets have included tortoises, which clattered in the bathtub, and parakeets, whose dander made me sneeze. Rabbits attracted hounds; lizards and their insect diets led to over-turned rocks in the garden border. A canary gave us a fright. Our most aggressive cat sprang from the stair and dislodged the cage. The door popped open, the bird popped out, and the cat nabbed it. Only Larry's presence kept the feline from looking like the cat that swallowed the canary.

Through their pets, the children learned nature's ways. The kids exercised care and compassion and grew up ecology-minded. We were selective; we avoided animals protected by law and rarely re-strained creatures that ordinarily roam free unless we found them hurt or abandoned by their parents. And we kept wild visitors for short periods of time.

Pets pose problems, of course. All animals, and especially wild and exotic ones, are health hazards; some (little green turtles, for example) are simply too risky. We insisted on cage-cleaning and hand-washing. Other minuses are cost, bother, and fail-ure of children to fulfill their promises. Even so, I feel that animals, carefully selected and properly handled, are worthwhile. Pets enrich children's lives and serve as centers of interest for family sharing.

* * *

We had many nature interests in addition to pets. Here are some suggestions for family activities.

Begin simply. Enjoy brilliant clouds at sunset; noisy migrating geese; seeds germinating on moist blotting paper; guppies in a bowl. Our "spectacu-lars" included a raucous pileated woodpecker that visited our biggest oak; a hummingbird nest on a pecan bough; a see-in nest that wasps built against a window pane. To share a sense of wonder, you don't need a degree in the life-sciences; indeed, you must guard against being too technical and detailed. Gear conversations to your child's age level and interests.

But encourage learning. The gray moss that hangs from trees became more interesting when someone told me it is a member of the pineapple family and contains chlorophyll. (Placed in water, the moss turns greenish.) Spice your conversations with fetching analogies and your child can comprehend complex ideas. Relate new information to the understood. Wonderful books are available in libraries and stores. Using a guidebook, I prefer to come upon an interesting specimen and look it up rather than go out and see how many plants or animals can be found and identified.

Don't be too directive. Allow your child to notice things and initiate conversation; on the other hand, interesting but inapparent features must sometimes be pointed out. Wonder out loud: "Why?" "How?"

Let the child teach you. Jennifer brought me an igneous rock. "Once the earth was a whirling glob of molten metal," I began my lecture. "I forget what the melted stuff is called—"

"It's called 'magma,'" Jennifer said. "We studied about it in school." Jennifer was in the first grade and full of surprises.

Later, at the beach, we found an empty slipper shell. I said it was half of a bivalve, but Jennifer insisted that the single shell was all there was—it was the complete home of a univalve creature.

"Then where did the little fellow live?" I demanded.

"In here." She pointed to a tiny cubbyhole.

This time I didn't feel so upstaged. Jennifer was in the fourth grade.

Be honest. If you don't know the answer, say so and invite, "Let's find out." Don't pump your child full of things he'll have to unlearn. In Larry's Sunday school class, the teacher gushed, "Isn't it nice of the lamb to give us wool!" Later, Larry saw sheep being shorn and saw that contributing to sweaters wasn't their idea.

Encourage reverence for life. Touring the Smithsonian Institution, we had admired human accomplishments, but then we came to ten large birds displayed in a glass case. With their heads cocked as if to eye us warily, they seemed very much alive, but they were dead—they and all their kind. They were passenger pigeons, and an explanatory plate related their fate. Once countless flocks numbering millions of birds swarmed over the United States. Hunting and land-clearing did them in. The last, Martha, died in captivity in 1914, and here she was, a monument to human avarice and unconcern.

"But daddy," Jennifer implored, her eyes as innocent as Martha's, "can't they grow some more?"

I explained that people, who themselves are a part of nature, can easily destroy what God has created. Some creatures, including the passenger pigeon, have been driven to extinction. Other animals are in peril. These include the great apes, condors, bald eagles, whooping cranes, desert sheep, and certain whales. I pointed to a new surge of interest in conservation but explained that some ecological issues are not easily resolved because of either conflicting interests or a lack of know-how or money.

My children were sadder but wiser as we resumed our tour.

Stress citizenship. Intent upon viewing the "secret" waterfall of friends, we boated to a remote lakeshore and then clambered up a tortuous path. When we arrived at the roaring cascade, we looked down into the crystal pool and saw a glinting object—a beverage can—and were crestfallen. It was a good occasion to talk about rights of others, including future generations. Larry proudly recalled an exemplary act performed by his brother. Randy took a friend to a drive-in restaurant and the girl threw a wrapper out the car window. Randy made her get out and retrieve it.

Emphasize basic principles. Stress that nature is amazingly orderly and dependable, although it isn't always gentle and must therefore be respected. Even snakes have their own gracefulness, and storms their fascination. Note relationships, causes and effects, growth and development. In some matters, nature will not be rushed. We waited all winter for our tadpole, Mr. Wiggly, to do his thing, and when he disappointed us judged him retarded. Then we learned that bullfrog tadpoles, unlike toad cousins, require a second year to mature. We released him in a nearby pond to finish growing up.

Assist in practical ways. Provide some equipment—magnifying glass, microscope, telescope or binoculars, camera, science kits. Help build a workbench, bird houses and feeders, compartmented box for minerals, glassed case for butterflies. Find space for a museum to house abandoned wasp nests, quartz-crystal castles, odd-looking seed pods. Encourage orderly collections and descriptive journals. Take field trips; don't neglect zoos, parks, farms, museums, aquariums, planetariums.

Be receptive. We are a hurrying people and we need to encourage our children to stop, look, and listen—to let nature speak to them so that they, in turn, may speak to themselves. I remember a family hike when we approached a great blue heron poised at the edge of a pond. The incredibly long neck extended so that the fiery eyes in the tiny head

　　　　　　　　　　　　　　A Father Shares

could scrutinize us. Reassured we meant it no harm, the bird took several mincing steps into the water as if disdaining to get its feet wet. Suddenly, the hosepipe-like neck flashed forward and the rapier beak speared a wriggling fish. Issuing coarse croaks, the heron lunged into the air and flapped away. It was a moment that said to us: "Be still, and know that I am God" (Ps. 46:10).

Sometimes when one of my children exclaimed, "Look, a cardinal!" I would be inclined to say, "A *cardinal*? We see them all the time." Instead, I remembered that each season I myself see a cardinal that seems brighter than any I have seen before, and I like to share such a moment.

We shared, and as my children watched blossoms unfold, I watched them unfold. Our conversations serve them well today and continue to enrich my own life.

An Everyday Religion

9

Jo and I were guests in a household of ten. At dinner our hostess smiled and said, "We're glad to have the Buggs with us."

"And happy Julie's home from college," her husband said.

"We're thankful for this great roast Mom cooked," chimed a son.

What a nice way to create the right mood for saying grace. But just then I heard the mother say "Amen." We weren't preparing for the blessing but celebrating it.

I coveted that naturalness but on reflection decided our own family's religious sharing has the same everyday quality. First, let me give some background.

As children and teen-agers, Jo and I were involved in church. Then (typically, I think) we took a holiday. But when Barbara came along, we wanted the best for her—and that included church. So we went.

Barbara fell in love with her teacher, and early on Sunday mornings, she pulled up in her crib, rattled the rails, and squealed, "Kunnie kool! Kunnie kool!" Although I had worked into the wee hours for the newspaper, I got up. That's the way we started— and each new child joined the procession. I sympathize with parents who have to hassle reluctant youngsters, but our children rarely resisted. Going to church was one of those things we regularly did together.

Christian education, at home and in church, began with stories linking God with love and creation, and picturing Jesus as caring friend (sometimes using familiar examples). We shared those interminable intercessions for mommy, daddy, brothers, sisters, grandparents, aunts, uncles, cousins, friends, pets, dolls. We said grace, sometimes holding hands. We tried family devotions, but individual meditations served us more dependably. Our richest sharing just happened.

After getting off late on a camping trip, we persevered through darkness, rain, and fog over the treacherous Blue Ridge Parkway to be confronted with a "Campground Full" sign. With the ranger's permission, we set up our tent-trailer in a parking area. While rain beat a tattoo on the canopy, we sat in lantern's glow enjoying sandwiches and hot chocolate. After supper, feeling thankful, I suggested devotionals and began reading from the Bible. A snicker—a giggle—and the trailer rocked with laughter. I scolded and began anew. More laughter. I was outraged. But then I recognized this was merely release from the tensions of our long journey.

"Let's pray," and I plunged on: "Dear God, you

An Everyday Religion 103

know how thankful we are for our family, the love we share, the good times we have together. We are most appreciative. Amen."

Jo and I gave leadership but considered nurture a two-way process. The children were close to God when they came into our family and seemed to stay that way. Our every-member-a-teacher concept shows in a Lenten experience:

Without fanfare, Randy began passing up dessert. To Larry, this meant his older brother was sick, physically or mentally. Larry swallowed his curiosity lest he jeopardize his extra portion but eventually asked what was going on.

"Randy's giving up desserts for Lent," Jo explained.

"I'd give up something but you wouldn't let me."

"What might that be?"

Our worldly angel shifted chocolate pie into his cheek. "School."

Jennifer, eight, said she was going to do what Randy was doing.

"Give up pie?" Larry asked incredulously.

"No, I'll decide on something different."

"Do you know why people do this?" I asked her.

"Sure. God gave up Jesus for us, so we give up things to be like him."

Impressed with her sincerity, I sent her to consult Randy. She returned and handed me her pledge:

"I will give up spending money except on Thursday and Saturday. I will spend only five cents on Thursday and Saturday. I will give up grapefruit. I will not buy any Rat Finks [toy creatures of plastic]. I will give up chewing gum."

"That's quite a list," I said appreciatively.

Next morning Jennifer found orange juice at her plate. She darted to the china cabinet behind me and I heard pencil-scratching. Then she sat down and asked for grapefruit.

Later, I chanced upon her pledge and found the grapefruit item marked through. In a subsequent amendment, she allowed herself one Rat Fink and two extra cents to spend each week. With those adjustments, she stuck to her commitments. Her self-denial reminded her of Christ's sacrificial life and death; it reminded Jo and me of the beautiful innocence and sincerity of the family's youngest member.

> And they were bringing children to him, that he might touch them; and the disciples rebuked them. But when Jesus saw it he was indignant, and said to them, "Let the children come to me, do not hinder them; for to such belongs the kingdom of God . . ." (Mark 10:13, 14).

Our God is not only approachable but also inclined to humor, even frivolity. Friends had us to lunch and their son suggested the "Johnny Appleseed Blessing." We sang lustily, then trailed off into silence.

"Pardon us, Lord," the lad apologized. "We'll be back in a minute." We dredged up the words and completed the blessing.

While acknowledging the need for ritual and order, I feel that we should encourage our children to be receptive to God's presence wherever and whenever and to feel rather free to celebrate. Visiting college students were presenting a program of testimony and song in our church.

"They're great," I whispered to Jo. "We ought to applaud."

"Then why don't you?"

"Because—" Because we are rather high-churchish, and in twelve years I had never heard applause during a worship service. My clapping would reverberate in that cavernous sanctuary, and hundreds of disapproving faces would turn to censure me. Still, I wanted to express my appreciation. If we were in an auditorium, I told myself, we wouldn't hesitate to show enthusiasm, so why discriminate against these young people because we happened to be in a church?

When the group finished, I smacked my hands together. For a split second, I was clapping solo—but then, a heavenly crescendo of applause.

On our way home, Larry, who had been in the choir, said, "Wasn't that clapping neat?"

"Yes," Jo said. "Do you know who started it?"

"Then it *was* dad. At the first clap, I whispered to Mike, 'That's got to be my daddy.'"

He was proud, and I was proud that he was proud.

When I sit in our congregation and look around me, I see scores of people who were like a father or mother, an older sister or brother, to our children. Our family would have been so much poorer without the teaching and preaching and range of programs—children's, youth, music, recreation, and others. The children were nurtured by caring ministry and supportive community. In such a moment of reflection, I feel a great sense of debt, and I find some comfort in the fact that each of us has made contributions.

Our family was instrumental in starting a camping program that is still going strong after sixteen years. We felt we could magnify the fun and benefits that we enjoyed camping with our own family by extending the circle to embrace our church family.

Every year (the first weekend following Mother's Day), twenty or so families gather in a private campground an hour's drive from Atlanta for a weekend camporee. The families bring their own shelter and their own food, which (except for two shared meals) they prepare at their own site.

We maintain a leisurely schedule to ensure informal sharing as we cluster at first one site and then another, getting acquainted and renewing friendships. Some spirited ball games and other group activities spring up. On Saturday night, we have a campfire. Sunday morning, pancakes are served from an army-surplus griddle, and then we move down to the lake for worship, with family or nature the theme. Warmed by fellowship and the morning sun, we feel close to God and one another. At noon, we have a potluck lunch.

On our buffet sits a silver bowl that our church gave us for being a representative exemplary family. Today the bowl reminds me of our children's heavy involvement in our church's life and outreach, and I'm glad we allowed them considerable latitude. Although we usually moved as a group in the current, each member was permitted to rock in eddies and reflect—or venture out and shoot newly discovered rapids. I knew that if I really believed that each child had to work out his/her own relationship with God, I had to support searching and testing. It wasn't always easy.

Larry became involved in a nondenominational youth group which I judged dogmatic, ingrown, and lacking in social welfare outreach, and I was tempted to pull him out of it. Instead, Jo and I accompanied him to parents' meetings, and the three of us came home and discussed our views.

I was pleased to see that Larry didn't abandon the trunk of his religious upbringing; instead, he added new branches: a richer acquaintance with, and love for, the Bible, and a comfortableness about sharing. The group afforded him a dependably accepting fellowship for this fermenting period of his life, and lasting friendships. Until he reviewed this manuscript, he wasn't fully aware of my misgivings about the group. "I'm glad you let me stay," he said. "Several families split when kids were ordered to drop out."

Youngsters have a better sense of what they need than we suppose. I recognize that browsing has its hazards and that some parents can point to tragic consequences; even so, I think risks must be taken—parental rigidity and intransigence can be even more costly. Understand, I'm not advocating turning babies loose in a cafeteria to feed themselves; I'm presuming the venturing youngster has had the benefit of a "core curriculum" of teaching in home and church.

But many children aren't being educated at all. Let's face it, the child who doesn't attend church school (or the equivalent) will likely grow up biblically illiterate. And some of those who do go will nonetheless be ill prepared (which suggests that parents should stay in touch). A friend of mine, responsible for a Lenten series for youth, decided to feature a dramatic presentation. "I drew blank stares," he related. "Many of those youngsters weren't vaguely familiar with the central events of Holy Week. I had to start from scratch."

We parents have primary responsibility for our children's spiritual development, but we cannot give what we don't possess. If we have convictions, we'll find ways to express them; if we don't, we'll bumble or remain silent. And we need consistency. John R. Bodo observes that we want to pass on something of the faith that has been our help in ages past and promises to be their hope for years to come; however, "there is something like a 90 percent inheritance tax on Christian faith." It helps, he says, if we will be as consistent as possible between our church life and family life. "If we parents don't seem to practice what the preacher preaches, the children will make short shrift of the preachment.

But if something of the love we profess in church . . . percolates into our family life, they will be less likely to give up the Christian faith, or even the institutional church . . ."

At the campfire of our last church camporee, Jo mentioned that only she, Larry, and I had attended all fifteen sessions. "If I can just get rid of the two of you," Larry quipped afterwards, "I will inherit the elder-statesman role."[1]

Larry's remark about inheritance aged me but cheered me. Our children's legacy is a spiritual foundation upon which they continue to build their own articles and practices of faith. We're in a great tradition, for families have played large roles throughout the history of God's people.

When little granddaughter Amy was baptized recently, I was swept by warm feelings. With nurture from Larry and Flo, she will grow up sensitive to God's presence and guidance. Already I've seen many fine qualities in Jake and Jody, Barbara's and Harold's boys. When they call and excitedly tell me about a Sunday school project, I recognize that we have come full circle from those days when Barbara roused us and demanded, "Kunnie kool!" I'm glad she got us started, and I'm glad we have kept going.

NOTE

[1]John R. Bodo, "Just What Can I Do for My Child?" *Presbyterian Life*, March 1, 1969, p. 4.

Welcome
to My World

10

Most men are so heavily invested in their careers that the job is their family's worst competitor. One happy solution is to bring family and work together.

When Barbara was still a toddler, I sometimes took her along on my reporting rounds. She flashed her hand and said "Hi!" to everyone, and people were friendly to her. A courthouse official gave her a snow-scene paperweight off his desk, and a policeman gave her a silver dollar. On hearing a siren, Barbara was like an old firehorse.

When I taught at Birmingham-Southern College, Jo often brought Barbara and Randy to the campus and joined me for lunch. Students and my colleagues made a fuss over the children.

Later, while I was on the *Atlanta Constitution* city desk, many Sunday afternoons Barbara and Randy

A Father Shares

rode a bus downtown and I met them and walked them to the paper. Staff members, including the late Ralph McGill, bought them Cokes, showed them the clattering teletypes, let them riffle through photos, and set them to typing "news stories." Sometimes the kids accompanied our reviewer to concerts or other entertainment.

I didn't question the propriety of these visits. For the children they were enjoyable, growing experiences. My youngsters were bright and well-mannered, and I was proud of them. They missed having me home Sunday afternoons, when most families are together, and the visits to the paper compensated. I would drive them home and we'd have supper as a family, and then I would return to work.

On-the-job sharing influences young lives and makes for rich memories. All twenty-five of the female candidates for the master of business administration degree at Harvard who were profiled in *The Managerial Woman* (by Margaret Hennig and Anne Jardim) recalled special times of sharing with their fathers. One remembered accompanying her dad, a railroad executive, on inspection trips:

> Sometimes we would ride on the work trains. They were always warm and smoky, filled with sweating and dirty men. I loved those times, and all the men knew me and talked to me. My dad was very proud of me and often joked with the men about my becoming the first woman train engineer. They would all laugh and then he would get very serious and say he didn't know what I would do but since I took after him I'd do something famous or unusual.[1]

Marjorie Holmes, author of best-selling inspirational books, went along with her father when he visited farms around Storm Lake, Iowa, buying chickens for the poultry house he managed. She recalls:

> Between jounces of the Model T, I scribbled my impressions of the countryside. At eight, I already knew what I wanted to be—a writer! Some of my sketches had been published in *Children's Activities*. Once, on a train, my dad chanced upon a copy and lurched through the car inviting, 'Read this. My little daughter wrote it.' Sam Holmes never met a stranger—if he did, he brought him (whole families even) home to dinner. That bald, stocky man had such a buoyant presence even the shyest people opened up to him. I'm glad he shared his company and himself with me. My desire to speak to readers concerning the things that matter most in their lives was planted and nurtured by my father.

Ward Patton, a Presbyterian minister, accompanied his dad on business trips. One winter when Ward was seven, the two of them drove up through north Florida and Georgia erecting signs that would direct truckers to the citrus plant where the father was employed. "I had never seen snow, and we kept watching the sky for some of that mysterious stuff," Ward recalls. "Meanwhile, dad made a game of practicing my multiplication tables. Those were fun times. The happiest part was knowing my dad wanted me with him."

Hugh Levin, an executive with Harry N. Abrams, publishers, says: "I was very close with my father [Martin Levin, who now heads book publishing for the Los Angeles Times-Mirror]. When I was three, my father took me on sales calls, and I would arrange his books in front of the competition on store shelves. Although in college I studied fine arts and architecture, it was inevitable I would pursue a career in books—I was prepared for it all my life."[2]

Another publishing executive, Roger Straus III of Harper & Row, had similar childhood experiences.

On Saturdays he would go to the office with his father, Roger, Jr., cofounder of what is now Farrar, Straus and Giroux. "After I had opened all the mail, my father would take me to a ball game—which was and continues to be a terrific way to be friends with your father. I shared his passion for publishing and never seriously thought about doing anything else."[3]

Some places of work are either unavailable or restricted, but all fathers can bring home news of the day's happenings—interesting people, challenging projects, humorous situations. It is tragic that many children have only a vague idea of what their father does for a living. Also, the parent can describe the world of work in positive ways so their child will not grow up apprehensive of the day when he himself will have to venture into the occupational realm.

Two cautions: Don't overwhelm or bore your youngster with complexities and details that he cannot appreciate, and don't feel crushed if he doesn't warm to your conversation—back off and try again another time. Also, don't oversell your organization and occupation; open the door to consideration of many careers and connections. On the other hand, don't block your child's inclinations to follow in your footsteps. Many young people find fulfillment pursuing the vocations of parents. Example: As a little girl, Phyllis Kravitch spent vacations traveling to courtrooms in the Savannah area with her attorney-father. Later, she went to law school and joined her dad in his practice. She recently became a U.S. appeals court judge.[4]

We lament the decline of family farms and shops, but there seems to be a resurgence in family businesses. I use a print shop where the parents, children, and in-laws work together in apparent harmony.

As women expand their perspectives and gain broader professional acceptance, we are seeing "John Public & Daughter" signs. Patti Capps, having finished college, asked her father for a job in his Searcy, Arkansas, auto dealership. He countered that his service manager might take her on, which he did. "You can't be a successful dealer," Patti observes, "if you've never had grease on your fingers." Similarly, Vera Groehler of Portland, Oregon, "always" wanted to work in her father's foundry. After taking engineering and business degrees, she began six-month apprenticeships in various parts of the plant, including the foundry itself, where she worked as a laborer. Later, she moved into the business office.[5]

Father-child partnerships have their pitfalls. Temperaments and value systems may clash. Some fathers view their child as immature and inexperienced; some children complain that their fathers are mossy reactionaries. Russell Jeckel, Illinois hog producer, and his father found themselves at odds.

> My father was conservative. Reliving the Depression, he feared another crash lurked around every corner. I was brash. I took a degree in vocational agriculture from the university and came home to be dad's partner. I had all the answers—I just might have tried to acquire all the individual hog houses in the state. We had violent arguments. "Take it easy," dad commanded. "You have a lifetime to get where you want to go."

> My wife and I took a plunge and bought sixteen commercial gilts. Although we lived in our hog houses that winter, disease took its toll. I began to see I was fortunate to have my dad applying brakes while I stoked; otherwise, I might have derailed. Now, as I relate to our five children, I have a better appreciation of my father, and I can see how his harsh background caused him to be cautious.

A Father Shares

I had a similar experience when my father enlisted me to succeed him as a weekly newspaper publisher. While I was still a college journalism student, I marked scores of corrections and suggestions on copies of my dad's papers, which I received in the mail. I had the audacity to send him those scarred pages. When I got into harness, I discovered that my father's willingness to let some things go even though imperfect was a key to the survival of the business. After a short while, I found the work too diverse and demanding, allowing little opportunity for polished writing and editing. Dad sold the papers for a good price, which persuades me to believe that fathers ought more often to liquidate their businesses rather than liquidate a reluctant son's or daughter's claims on happiness.

I have so far stressed career-related sharing between father and child, but a variety of other opportunities are available, including sports, hobbies, travel, church and community activities, and household chores.

In *Father Feelings*, Eliot Daley, a minister who is a member of the "Mister Rogers' Neighborhood" staff, says he is less concerned about frequenting his children's world of fun and games than he is about making his own life available to them:

> To enable them to find out anything they want to know about me, for instance. What I do at work. How I treat people. How I plan and execute jobs. How I handle pressure. What I get out of it.
>
> Or to involve them in any decision-making that affects them—and even some that does not— because I value their opinions. Or to be honest with them about family tensions, and exchange candid feedback about how we're living our life together.[6]

I have actively sought to enlarge my children's world by inviting them into my own. It has been my privilege to acquaint them with important people—and some who are important only because they are interesting. I differ with experts on etiquette and child-rearing who suggest feeding children apart from dinner guests. Allowing for tender years and conflicting schedules, I believe youngsters should, as a rule, join adults at the table and shouldn't bolt as soon as dessert is consumed. At the table, children absorb information and insights, learn to relate to strangers, improve their conversation, refine their graces, and may make contacts that will be of practical value later. By welcoming their children, the parents say, "You belong. I trust you." On the other hand, "Shoo, this is adult!"—even when said with a smile—can be demeaning. As for the guests, I can only surmise that many enjoy, as I do, getting acquainted with the hosts' children.

Exchanges with adults, both in the home and in the community, enhance the development of social conscience and responsible behavior. We cannot precisely predict our children's future needs, but they will no doubt include understanding, compassion, and a desire to serve. The love that is experienced in the home will overflow into the community.

We complain about the invasion of peer influences, and with justification, because peer cultures can be shallow and destructive. But some fathers invoke peer pressures as an excuse for their own failures to share. Professor Urie Bronfenbrenner, the Cornell University development authority, says we aren't as helpless as we assume. He believes that kids are more often turned off by parental inattention than they are turned on by a preference for members of their own age group. He says young-

A Father Shares

sters hear the adult world saying: "Don't bug us, latch onto your peers!"

You don't want a cloying togetherness which gives rise to dependency, but vibrant caring and sharing. "We need to bring adults back into the lives of children, and children back into the lives of adults," Dr. Bronfenbrenner declares.[7]

We need to say, "Welcome to my world."

NOTES

[1]See Acknowledgments.

[2]Adapted from Thomas Weyr, " 'Second Generation' Is Making Its Own Imprint in Publishing," *Publishers Weekly,* April 16, 1979, p. 33.

[3]Adapted from Weyr, p. 33.

[4]"Little Judge Again Makes History," Barbara Moran, *Atlanta Journal,* Feb. 1, 1979, p. 1B.

[5]"Fathers Hiring Daughters," *New York Times,* in *Atlanta Constitution,* Aug. 27, 1976.

[6]See Acknowledgments.

[7]Urie Bronfenbrenner, "Parents Bring Up Your Children!" *Look,* Jan. 26, 1971, p. 45. Excerpted from *Two Worlds of Childhood; U.S. and U.S.S.R.* (Russel Sage Foundation, 1970). Also, interview with Susan Byrne, "Nobody Home: The Erosion of the American Family," *Psychology Today,* May 1977, p. 41. Adapted from *Who Cares for America's Children?* an interview tape (Science Interface, 1977).

Get Your
Own Act
Together

My father rarely unburdened himself of his
weekly newspaper duties, so mother and I made
our excursions to the city (Birmingham) without
him.

Some conductors considered themselves doing
passengers a favor by letting them board, and these
demanded "Tickets!" imperiously. I shrank into the
plush upholstery when mother proffered the yellow packet that shouted we were not paying
passengers but were riding on that contemptible
script, received in exchange for advertising. That
endless ribbon of coupons was sure to stream out of
the conductor's hand like a novelty-store trick,
earning his wrath.

Jackson's Gap—Alexander City—Kellyton—
Goodwater—Sylacauga. It was time to get out the
shoe box packed with goodies—sandwiches, fried

chicken, deviled eggs, and cake. Even at five, I knew water wasn't the beverage of tourists, and when the news butch came hawking frosty pop, I tugged at mother's sleeve but readily acknowledged that fifteen cents was an outrage. At Berkstresser Brothers Drug Store, you got Coca-Cola in a glass of ice for a nickel.

In the hotel where we stayed on due bill, I rode the elevators for hours on end, and then mother and I had supper out of the box. I propped on a window sill and marveled at the sights and sounds of downtown Birmingham. When I grew sleepy, mother and I piled up in bed and she told me great stories.

Next morning, we visited all the toy departments. By noon, I would have made my selection and we'd go into a restaurant, order soft drinks, and sneak out our box and consume its remnants. Glares from waitresses and managers gave me my first practice in appearing nonchalant.

Afternoons were anticlimaxes trailing mother as she tried on hats and consulted cosmeticians. The time would elude us and we would hasten toward the train station. Almost there, it would happen. "Lordy, honey, I left my purse in the ladies' room at Loveman's." Back we'd go, retrieving the lost item or not, then run for the train. I can still feel that suitcase swinging me sideways.

Relieved to catch the train, we didn't mind undergoing the script indignity anew. We reversed a seat to make a double, propped up our weary feet, and munched on coconut macaroons from the dime store and swigged one of those extravagant grape sodas.

"Mother, when can we do this again?"

"Soon maybe. Would you like that?"

"Oh, yes ma'am," I chortled. I rested my head on my mother's shoulder and gazed out the window.

With the rails clicking and the coach swaying, I soon would be asleep.

* * *

"I shouldn't have left home. None of the Buggs ever amounted to anything. If your daddy had half my daddy's business sense, I wouldn't be living in rooms and skimping."

"Daddy says anybody could do well if they inherited twenty-five thousand dollars," I protested.

"Hush! There you go, siding with your father again."

" 'Cause you're talking mean."

"Shut up! If my brothers had sassed my mother, my daddy would have knocked them clean across the room. But your father—"

"Well, I love him better'n I love you!"

"So this is what I get for tearing up my insides. I wish you'd never been born."

"I didn't ask to be born!" I retorted.

The broom struck me across the shoulders and the handle splintered. Mother grabbed up the fire poker but already I was out of range running out the front door. I leapt off the porch and raced for the asylum of my father's print shop.

* * *

I had two mothers, one cuddling and companionable, the other agitated and abusive. Mother suffered spells of discontent, and I reminded her of the pain and sacrifices that she associated with marriage and parenthood.

Assured a college education, mother dropped out because of an illness. She fell in love with a young man who soon died unexpectedly and mysteriously. Perhaps she expected my father to replace both her fiancé and her father; if so, he did not fulfill her expectations.

Dad came out of harsh poverty to earn a

A Father Shares

bachelor's degree at thirty-five and then a master's. After a stint as a school principal, he bought a decrepit weekly newspaper, worked day and night, and built a successful business. With his spartan background, dad was a practical man of simple tastes and few wants. He was dedicated to his principles and could be quite impatient with people holding clashing views. He was compassionate but awkward at showing affection. He had no use for frivolity and little use for the arts.

In contrast, mother was an extravagant romantic. She could sketch, paint, play the piano, sing, do readings, write skits, act, and direct. She gladly played the fool, delighting children and fun-loving adults. She practiced good works, but her relationships tended to be tenuous. An inconsistency was counseling married couples—strange when her own marriage was rocky and unfulfilling.

My earliest recollections of mother contrast sharply. When I was four, she had twins who lived only hours. I stayed with an aunt. I picked violets and carried them to mother. The other setting was our kitchen table. During a violent argument, mother picked up a butcher knife and slashed dad's hand. I was horrified and angry. These memories capsule the tempestuous love-hate relationship that my mother and I would have.

When mother became emotionally overcharged, she threw herself upon her bed, cried in anguish, shook violently, and beat upon herself with her fists. These spells frightened and grieved me, but when I tried to comfort her, she seemed unaware of my presence. As I grew older, I was more often the target of her rage. "Someday you'll understand," my dad said, but I didn't think I would ever understand.

I couldn't please mother. Even after my marriage, I was harassed by her criticism. We shouldn't have bought a new refrigerator, shouldn't be having another baby. I flared at the slightest provocation. We fared best when our visits were short and infrequent.

Fourteen years ago, mother was killed in an automobile accident. Gone was the mother whom I loved in spite of the brittleness of our relationship; gone were my chances for reconciliation. I wanted to cry out: "Mother, come back! I'm not through talking with you. I want to know you and have you understand me. I want to forgive and be forgiven!" In *Who Is Sylvia?*, author Lucy Freeman describes similar feelings over the death of her mother, who somehow wasn't able to share the love that the daughter wanted and needed. She writes: "I still deeply mourn my mother. Part of me always will. I am haunted by the tragedy of her life, the sorrow in those sapphire eyes. But most of all I mourn her inability to convey to me her feelings all those years. And my inability to let her know what I felt. Not the hate. That she knew. But the love."[1]

Even in death, my mother would continue to dominate me. Fortunately, I had already begun restructuring my self-image and behavioral patterns two years before mother died. In this campaign to find sufficient inner strength to become my own person, my first and biggest step was to quit my newspaper job.

My first six years on the paper were happy ones. I was learning, growing, advancing. But then I began feeling jaded, overworked, put upon. I lost confidence in the employee policies and practices; saw no opportunity for advancement (and no job that I wanted); hated working for a superior who threw tantrums; and missed being home with my family nights and holidays. I suffered depressions along with a series of vague discomforts that my doctor attributed to "nerves."

A Father Shares

Although I was ruining my personality and health and straining my relationships, for six years I stayed and stewed. I had some legitimate justifications: I was forty-one; I had six mouths to feed and four minds to educate; and I was indentured to a mortgage that had an immortality complex. But mostly I was imprisoned by self-doubt.

At home, someone was sure to say or do the wrong thing, whereupon I would explode. Afterward, I would retreat to our bedroom and stay there for hours, days, weekends. Jo would beg me to rejoin the family: "You are a good, kind person. You have lots of friends; you're respected at the paper; the children and I love you dearly. Come and be with us." But I would grovel deeper in self-contempt and pity. Why try again? Didn't I always fail? I couldn't get along with people because I was a misfit, a congenital misfit. How could anyone, including God, expect normal behavior from someone who had suffered so much emotional neglect and abuse?

We went on a church retreat. New friends listened to me; more importantly, they encouraged me to listen to myself. For the first time, I was able to accept myself as a person of value and potential. I didn't have to do my thing in order to prove my worth—I was okay as a gift of God's grace.

I resolved to rebuild my life consistent with the new identity that was emerging, and my job seemed the place to start. Jo and I decided I would stick with it six months, then quit and try free-lancing. Sixteen years later, I'm still free-lancing.

My work was just one of my problems, but breaking away was a rite of passage that gave me courage to assume responsibility for my attitudes and behavior generally. I became more reasonable, philosophical, trusting, appreciative. Where I'd been shouting "No!" to life because it seemed to shake its head negatively at me, I said "Yes!" It was a glorious feeling.

But a sore place remained: my relationship with mother. While writing an autobiographical book, *Job Power* (on careers, now out of print), I recognized that I had encouraged readers to bury destructive elements of their past and yet I had not buried my pain over my mother. I blamed my moodiness on her capriciousness, and although I had softened my depressions, I resented this terrible legacy. I had chopped down the tree of my relationship with mother and bulldozed it from the center of my consciousness, but while revising my book I kept circling the stump and stumbling over the awful roots.

One day as I stared at my typewriter, release surged through me. The resentment and guilt evaporated; my mind turned clear and my muscles relaxed. In a transformation that was at once an insight, a confession, and a commitment, I was ready to make peace with mother. I saw why my attempts at reconciliation had failed. It wasn't a lack of charity; I could have managed that; rather, I needed to keep this burden on my back. It was my certification as a cripple. If I began walking upright and free, people would expect—even demand— that I behave responsibly. I had kept the wounds open and stoked the grudges to escape blame for inexcusable behavior.

In a cleansing process, I projected the films of my life with my mother onto the screen in my mind. I snipped out frames that I wished to preserve and burned the rest. I kept pictures of a mother who kissed away childhood hurts and made illness bearable. Who spent a great deal of time with me, often when my father was either too busy or lacked the inclination. Who entertained me with stories, games, sketches, paper dolls, stuffed animals, and

　　　　　　　　　　A Father Shares

shoe-box peep shows. Who shared gifts that my dad didn't have and couldn't give: an eye for beauty, a flair for the dramatic, a love of fun, a readiness to perform in public—aptitudes that enrich my work and leisure. I also cherish her for becoming a second mother to Jo after Mrs. Smith died, and for loving her grandchildren and brightening their lives in countless ways.

Reconciliation continues. In addition to focusing on good things my mother did *for* me instead of the bad things she did *to* me, I have reconstructed possible causes of her discontent and rage. Like me, she probably had an unbearable self-contempt (although she never acknowledged it). As with me, something in her childhood was out of kilter. I suspect that her parents indulged her whims, seldom opposed her wilfulness, and generally dealt with her as being impossibly high-strung and immature, and she may have believed they didn't take her seriously or respect her as a complete person. I also appreciate her misfortunes: illnesses and surgery and hypochondria; loss of infant twin daughters; financial struggles; misgivings about her marriage and her relationship with me; my father's stroke, commitment to the state mental hospital, and death two years later; and a terrible wreck preceding the fatal one. Even with good health and good fortune, mother might have related to me poorly, but certainly the bad breaks exacerbated her frustrations and her self-concern.

I believe I have made peace with mother, but some may say that my feelings, as I have expressed them, refute this. One reviewer of Christina Crawford's *Mommie Dearest* marveled that the abused adopted daughter of Joan Crawford could be so mild-mannered and forgiving, but another said, "She's still furious."[2] I continue to have ambivalent feelings, but don't we all? I have come a long way.

Last Mother's Day, I wore a rose for my mother. It was the first time in my adult life that I had gladly worn this symbol in the intended spirit of love and appreciation.

These experiences are painful to write about, and some readers may be annoyed at such intensely personal sharing. Reynolds Price, the novelist, decries the spate of "my parents don't love me" books. He says the authors encourage us to assign all our woes to parents who weaned us on "the gruel of neglect" and to invoke our parents' inadequacies as a universal alibi for failing to love another person, or failing to brush our teeth, or not pulling up our socks and becoming a competent person. He says it's odd by comparison that one of the Ten Commandments exhorts children to honor their parents, and not vice versa.[3] [He neglects: ". . . What man of you, if his son asks him for bread, will give him a stone? Or if he asks for a fish, will give him a serpent? (Matt. 7:9, 10)"]

Pulling up your socks will be an empty gesture if you don't first deal with that gruel of neglect, real or imagined. Many angry and disconsolate persons can't bring themselves to *think* about their negative feelings, much less explore them and assume responsibility for their reactions. We must will ourselves to be free, it's true, but most of us will not be able to muster a great surge of resolve and extricate ourselves; first, we have to deal decisively with the muck—if we don't, we will continue to get stuck in it and track it into our homes.

Many grown men and women are languishing in the imprisoning shadow of a father or mother, alive or dead. There is a universal bone-marrow-deep craving to be close to our parents. In *Finding My Father*, Rod McKuen, who was born out of wedlock, describes his search for the father he had never known. He wanted a feel for this man who gave him

A Father Shares

life; beyond this, he wanted to reach out and say, "Look, Dad, everything turned out okay."[4] In contrast, most of us are afforded geographical proximity, but this does not assure closeness. Georges Simenon, whose phenomenal productivity as a writer of mysteries may have come from a need to prove himself to his mother, wrote *Letter to My Mother* three years after her death at age ninety-one. "You brought me into the world," he said. "I came out of your womb, you gave me my first milk, and yet I didn't know you any more than you know me."[5] Although Joan Crawford persisted in treating Christina cruelly, the daughter kept coming back—as child, teenager, adult—hoping to find mutuality. She explains her quest in terms of the legendary Lorelei and "the sound of a lullaby buried deep in our past."

As Reynolds Price suggests, many of our expectations are unrealistic and selfish, but this is more reason for reconciliation—we must bring our fantasies into the light of reality. Nancy Friday (*My Mother, My Self*) says she had to correct "this illusion of perfect love between my mother and me."[6] My own fallacy was blaming mother—on and on—for my continuing failure to rise to my potential as a person. My choice to remain dependent was my own.

What I needed wasn't more guilt—I already stood convicted in my own eyes. No matter how many times someone might have shouted, "Honor your mother!" I couldn't have pulled it off. My recovery required a miracle—the miracle of reconciliation. In the process, the focus shifted from mother to me. I had to say, "Sure, it was like that, but I'm not going to spend the rest of my life being curator of a museum of horrors; I have more important things to do. If I keep on punishing mother, I keep abusing myself. I don't want that. Through the grace of

God, I will find new ways to understand, forgive and forget, appreciate, and even love."

If you have a rotten relationship, some garbage from it is sure to spill over into your other relationships, especially your life with your children. Any chronic alienation—from a neighbor, the preacher, the school system, or the world generally—can contaminate your relationship with your children. But the chief offenders, I believe, are problems with your own parents, your marriage, and your job.

I have described how my feud with mother caused me to be anxious, self-protective, easily slighted or rebuffed. I lashed out—sometimes physically, always emotionally. Dr. Benjamin Spock says, "The strongest impulse in a human being is to repeat the pattern set by parents." I repeated the behavior that I despised.

As to marriage, although Jo and I have enjoyed a good one, there have been times when we nursed hurts and failed to resolve conflicts, or felt thwarted or inadequate sexually. Our negative moods rippled through the household, and our children had difficulty dealing with these episodes. The problem would have been intensified if Jo and I had tried to recruit allies, or let the children play one of us against the other, or belittled each other as persons. Another redeeming factor: the children knew that we had an abiding love. If we fathers want our children to aspire to—and contribute to—happy, healthy marriages, we must serve as believable models. And if, in spite of our efforts, our marriage fails, the disruption may increase the need for constructive behavior.

My job poisoned my family relationships. It, too, kept me feeling tentative, inadequate, and antagonistic. If I had continued to be gloomy, my children might have developed fears of the world of work, and later they might have allowed themselves to remain in jobs that caused them to feel unhappy and empty—jobs they have ditched. Work addiction is likewise a problem. By definition, the work addict's values are skewed. He may regard work as man's reason for being; even if he doesn't love his job, he may see in it his best chances for feeling fulfilled. Exposed to this behavior, children, too, may develop warped priorities. And there is a sinister possibility: the father, recognizing that his family feels bereft, may attempt to prevent them from also feeling resentful by pretending to hate his work—he is fighting a dragon in his family's behalf. Such behavior may cause children to feel confused and guilty.

Life is complex and demanding, and all relationships undergo strain from time to time and may even buckle. But you *can* rise above your frustrations, hostility, and remorse. Take stock. What kinds of negative feelings beset you? Who and what precipitate these feelings? What are the real meanings of these conflicts or disappointments?

Once you understand what's happening inside you, you are in a better position to deal with the problems. You may wish to apologize and make amends—in any case, you can be more understanding, more philosophical. Tell yourself you can't afford the hurt or anger. You may need to reduce your exposure to the precipitating person or situation, and to release tension through recreation and other activities.

If the destructive source lies in the past, remember that the past cannot devastate you unless you allow it. You cannot prevent disturbing memories from popping into your head, but you can learn to neutralize and dismiss them.

Your family wants to be supportive when you are undergoing strain outside the home, so don't be secretive—if you clam up, they may feel they're the culprits. On the other hand, don't overdramatize. Don't parade your wounds, villify your adversaries, or push your children into a no-man's-land between you and the "enemy." That's dumping garbage.

You can employ a variety of coping devices, but to make lasting peace with others, you have to make peace with yourself and with God. The life and teachings of Jesus have helped sustain me. The good news is that each of us is a unique person having infinite value and possibilities, capable of surmounting the worst of beginnings and overcoming crises as they arise. Moreover, other persons, too, are entitled to be different—and to be loved.

By getting my own act together, I became a better father, better person. I wish the change had come earlier—but I must not allow myself to be victimized by that ghost, either. It's never too late. Now that my children and I relate voluntarily rather than on a survival basis, it's good we aren't mired in all that garbage.

NOTES

[1]Recommended: Howard Halpern, *Cutting Loose: An Adult Guide to Coming to Terms with Your Parents* (Simon and Schuster, 1976).

[2]Lucy Freeman, *Who Is Sylvia?* (Arbor House, 1979), p. 302.

[3]The references are to Christina Crawford, *Mommie Dearest* (William Morrow, 1978; Berkley paperback).

[4]Reynolds Price, review of *Farther Off from Heaven* by William Humphrey, *New York Times Book Review*, March 27, 1977, p. 7.

[5]Rod McKuen, *Finding My Father: One Man's Search for Identity* (Cheval/Coward, McCann and Geoghegan, 1967; Berkley paperback).

[6]Georges Simenon, *Letter to My Mother*, trans. Ralph Manheim (Harcourt, Brace, Jovanovich, 1976), p. 64.

[7]Nancy Friday, *My Mother, My Self* (Delacorte, 1978; Dell paperback).

[8]"The Family: Holding Its Own in a Period of Changing Values," *New York Times*, Aug. 5, 1973, p. 54.

Father Knows Best?

12

"You do *what*?" I was incredulous.

"As I read the morning paper," my friend said, "I take a felt pen and blot out any words that might corrupt my daughter."

"And she's how old?"

"Seventeen."

Wall in the innocent child; wall out the worldly world. Compared with hand-to-hand combat, it's an approach having simplistic appeal. Throw out the television; tell the mother of the foul-talking child to keep him on their side of the street; decree (while daughter is still in her stroller) there will be absolutely no dates until sixteen, then guard her until you can ship her off to a "safe" college.

Walls may insulate, but they have shortcomings:

• There'll be leaks. Junior will watch TV elsewhere.

• You can't keep a kid inside an anti-shark cage forever.

• Instead of separating your child from the world, you may estrange him from yourself.

• A single fence looks so frail, you build another—and another. Soon you're behind a Maginot Line.

I'm not advocating letting kids run hog-wild or contriving ways to season them. Concerning a given situation, a child may lack the necessary insights, experience, skills, resiliency. For example, parents who work outside the home ask for trouble when they allow youngsters to flock there after school.

What I'm urging is a positive and constructive climate in which every individual's integrity and dignity are respected. The practice of honesty and compassion equips children for rich and responsible living; in contrast, a distrustful and authoritarian atmosphere tends to produce persons who will be naive, judgmental, and easily frustrated. Often parents assume that they know intuitively what's best for the child, but I've learned the hard way that fathers (mothers) don't *always* know best.

Here are guidelines I've come by:

1. Be willing to listen as well as talk, to discuss as well as issue edicts.

2. Understand the issue. Don't press cures for nonexistent diseases. What is the child's position? How intense are his feelings? Be alert for unexpressed feelings.

3. Expressing himself allows the child to organize and evaluate his own information and reasoning.

4. Don't cheat the child out of growth he might experience by acting responsibly on a voluntary basis.

5. On matters that aren't negotiable, say no after

Father Knows Best? 133

minimal discussion. State your position succinctly and in the least threatening way. Then don't vacillate—your child will find your decision harder to live with; and don't grovel in guilt—your child will find *you* harder to live with.

6. Some issues should be considered jointly with father and mother. Don't let a child play one parent against the other.

7. Avoid mixed messages—example: your words and tone conflict.

I've gathered these principles from failures as well as successes. Here are several of my experiences:

Barbara asked for a graduation ring. We didn't have the money to spare, but instead of saying that (she would have graciously yielded), I ridiculed the ring as an overpriced bauble. At breakfast several days later, Jo reminded me that orders had to be placed that day.

"Barbara, how badly do you want this thing?" I demanded. "Are you willing to help pay for it out of your summer earnings?"

"No," she said coolly.

"Well, if that's the way you feel, let's just forget the whole thing!"

Barbara left in tears. The ensuing silence told me we weren't going to forget. "Jo," I complained, "why didn't you come right out and say you wanted her to have the ring?"

"I don't know. I just wish we didn't always have to put a price on everything."

On reflection, I saw that Jo and I had responded out of our divergent experiences. Although Jo's parents could afford few frills, they insisted that she have a ring. In contrast, I could have had one, but I dismissed it as a trinket. I hadn't checked into Barbara's sentiments, but she probably viewed the ring as a symbol of family appreciation for attainment by one of its members. Remembering how considerate and frugal Barbara had been, I felt cheap for having given her a "money doesn't grow on trees" lecture.

"She should have the ring," I said to Jo. I wrote a check, then attempted a note to be left with it in the principal's office. I tore up several drafts which intimated "We'll buy the ring, even though it's expensive, but next time try to be more considerate." Then I got it right: "Dearest Barbara, we want you to have the ring as a token of our love and appreciation. Devotedly, Mother and Daddy."

Next morning, Barbara rewarded me with a big kiss. She dismissed my efforts to apologize. "Everything's okay, really."

Later, Jo told me that Barbara had brought the check home and insisted that the money be applied toward camp for Larry. "I had to insist before she would return to school and place the order. But she'll enjoy the ring so much. And, you know, I sense a new ring of love around our family."

Sometimes I was much too conscious of the burden of responsibility that comes with the "Parent" badge. Like the time when Jo caught me staring down at my plate and asked me what was wrong.

"Nothing," I said, toying with my peas, which I was contemplating in order to avoid looking at Larry's long hair and the sickly fuzz he fondly called a moustache. Why had he done it? He'd been so handsome!

My contemporaries scorned long hair as being a symbol of the hippie rebellion, but Larry insisted that his hair wasn't a social statement but a personal preference. Even Randy, who sometimes thought me a bit strict, said the moustache ought to come off. "It isn't appropriate for a high-school kid," said the collegian, fingering his own beard.

When a neighbor blurted, "Larry, you look just

like a girl!" I was tempted to issue the edict. Still, I didn't want to do Larry an injustice or estrange us, so I held my fire. We talked about long hair—but on other boys' heads. A friend was strong-armed into a barber chair by his father.

"That wasn't right," Larry declared.

I agreed.

"A person has a right to wear his hair the way he likes."

I wasn't sure and said nothing. But I became sensitive to parental impositions. A mother importuned her daughter to show me her new orthodontic braces, and when the girl refused, she pried open her mouth as a trader might handle a horse.

In time, we went to Ocracoke on vacation. One noonday I was sitting under our canopy contemplating Larry, who was flying a kite, and I suddenly became aware of his hair. During the last three days, we had set up camp together, fished together, played cards together, and his hair had escaped my consciousness. In that moment, I recognized that what had bothered me back home wasn't *Larry's* appearance but my own. I didn't want my peers to judge me uncaring or ineffective as a father. With that insight, I quit fretting about the hair and a lot of other things. (Strange, but now when we view our Ocracoke slides, I see that Larry's hair wasn't all *that* long.)

I handled crises better than petty annoyances. (Was that because the child usually was penitent and I felt needed?)

Larry called me from school. "Dad, can you come and get me?"

"Yes, son. Are you sick?"

"No, sir, I've been suspended for two days."

The drive to school was two miles, and I counted to ten a number of times. On the way home, Larry said he had put a tack in another boy's chair. But why?

"He put a tack in my chair first. It hurt!"

"Did you explain that to the teacher?"

"No! I'm not going to rat on anybody!"

There is honor among thieves and pranksters, an admirable trait, and yet this latest disturbance of the peace couldn't be shrugged off. How does a father convey the gravity of an infraction without implying that the world is coming to an end? How does he show he detests the offense but loves the offender? And does a father acknowledge that he himself got into scrapes, but expects better of his son?

Somehow, I found the right language to express my disappointment, and I arrived at a sentence that was tempered with mercy.

Later I passed Larry's room and saw him lying on his bed, his head buried in his pillow. I went in and massaged his back. "Larry, I love you very much."

He rolled over and smiled, and the cost of being a father—so high half an hour earlier—no longer seemed exhorbitant.

* * *

In chapter 5, I talked about the discrepancy between those "pictures in our heads" and our children as they are. I remember Frances Statham, author of historical romances, saying she loves her heroes because "They are the only men who will do precisely what I want them to do." Similarly, we make puppets of our children even though we recognize, intellectually, that they must be allowed to make mistakes.

"Don't expect too much of your child, and don't feel he must see you as perfect," advises Henry Biller, University of Rhode Island psychologist. "That is stifling to both of you. You don't have to have the last word. There's a big difference between a father who is wishy-washy and one who listens to rational argument and sometimes gives in." In *Father Power*, Biller and coauthor Dennis Meredith counsel dads not to try to cloak their failings but rather impress upon their children that a normal person has faults "but that these do not have to affect his overall happiness or competence as a human being." On the other hand, fathers shouldn't belittle themselves or their children, Biller and Meredith note.[1]

William K. Zinsser, writer, is grieved that the American dream is a dream of getting ahead, emblazoned in gold wherever we look. By insisting that every next step be a step upward, we paralyze our young people.

> "But what if we fail?" they ask, whispering the dreadful word across "the generation gap" to their parents, who are back home at the Establishment, nursing their "middle-class values" and cultivating their "goal-oriented society." The parents whisper back: "Don't!" What they should say is "Don't be afraid to fail!" Failure isn't fatal. Countless people have had a bout with it and come out stronger as a result.[2]

Our children require our acceptance and approval, but praise isn't easily given or received. The *over*praised youngster becomes hooked on applause—acclaim is more important than the satisfaction of mastering, creating, accomplishing. Oddly, a lack of attention produces virtually the same result. A hospitalized eight-year-old, burned by gasoline set afire during play, wanted to know, "Are the other kids talking about it?

Parents show their children off shamefully. A friend trained her little sister to spell "Constantinople" and "hippopotamus." She recalls: "I would set her in the midst of guests and have her spell those two words. Then I hustled her away before someone could ask her to spell 'cat.' " Parents, too, seek empty applause for their children (and themselves).

Overdemanding/overpraising parents drive their children to cheat, lie, steal. Example, a first-grader was bringing home beautiful art work. But it wasn't hers. When her first few pictures drew criticism at home, she began borrowing a classmate's. This same child put her head on her desk and cried: "But I don't want a 96! My mom expects me to make 100."

Here's how to corrupt your child's values and behavior:

• Demand performance beyond his capabilities and motivation.

• Emphasize grades and publicity rather than accomplishment.

• Allow your child to run with the "wrong crowd."

• Imply that the worst crime is to get caught.

• Shame him by discussing his misbehavior in front of others. Call him "stupid." Talk "around" him as though he weren't present.

• Berate him as a person rather than criticize his behavior. Scream at him, shake him, say you wish he'd never been born and you may give him away. Threaten that God or the devil or a policeman will get him.

• Invariably take the side of authorities.

• Fail to discuss the harm of immoral and dishonest practices; fail to set examples of facing up to problems and acting responsibly. Cheat on your taxes. Lie about your child's age. Keep excess change. Shrug, "It's a big corporation—nobody gets hurt."

• Let problems slide. "Life's more pleasant without hassles." (Gallows laugh.)

• Be afraid of your child. Worse, let him know it.

• Assume that it's too late for improvement.

A reader, forgetting, may protest, "You make it sound easy, but you just don't know my Billy!"

But I do know what it is like to try one form of discipline after another and yet fail. We have to persist; we have no option. We have to try to lead and persuade, and when necessary invoke sanctions of the sternest sort. As Carol Burnett shared, following her daughter's drug addiction and recovery: love does not require you to accept destructive behavior.

Discipline isn't easily designed, and it's often painful to apply. I'm glad that, except for an occasional mild rebuke to a grandchild, I have graduated. We aren't born expert and few of us, for all our experience, ever earn the title "authority." We recognize that we will not perform perfectly; even so, we can aspire to act responsibly, employing patience, wisdom, and courage.

At the close of an exasperating day, you wonder about the quiet in the boys' room. Through the cracked door, you spy the five-year-old drawing people on the new wallpaper with a lipstick. The three-year-old is whirling around with a marking pen in an outstretched hand. You burst in and give them your meanest stare. The awful quiet is broken when the little one, with subdued pride, declares, "I drew the roads."

What do you do? You do what you must, hopefully in a context of love and in anticipation of better days when you will be shown respect and affection, as in this scene:

A friend was icing her husband's birthday cake. Their first-grader wandered in, propped on the kitchen table, and ever so mousily flicked off a bit of icing and tasted it.

"You'd better not get into this cake!" his mother scolded. "If you do, your daddy will skin you alive."

"No, mother," he said softly. "Cake isn't that important to my daddy."

NOTES

[1]Biller and Meredith, *Father Power* (McKay, 1974), pp. 110–11.
[2]William K. Zinsser, "Looking Around with Zinsser: The Right To Fail," *Look,* Oct. 17, 1967, p. 10.
[3]See n. 5, c. 5.

Pink or Blue,
Intimately You

13

After a trusted neighbor made sexual advances toward a little friend of ours, Jo said she would counsel Jennifer, age eleven, to be cautious, but I suggested that I do it. "Perhaps I—a man—can persuade her this isn't representative male behavior."

It wasn't easy talking to Jennifer, but I wasn't terribly embarrassed. In our family, sex is an integral part of life. With two boys and two girls, anatomical differences were apparent and accepted. We began talking about sexuality early, taking cues from each child's age and interests. Often I capitalized on an encounter with pets or wildlife.

Larry and I discovered immature beetles in a rotted log and we talked about ways nature protects babies. Some are shielded in their mother's body—Larry was. Similarly, Jennifer and I watched a squirrel feverishly cutting boughs for a nest. I remarked that Jo had prepared for Jennifer's arrival with that same urgency, and someday Jennifer might experience this expectation. Additionally, many times "Doctor" Barbara supervised her young obstetrical team in behalf of kittens and puppies.

Parents have the ultimate responsibility for their children's sex educations, which should begin early and be broad, reliable, balanced, honest, and continuing. But they need all the help they can get, and we were fortunate to have an outstanding program in our church. Each year, a series of seminars—lectures, films, and discussions on all aspects of sexuality—was presented to students in grades seven through twelve. Unlike scare programs, ours stressed basic values including self-respect and social concern. We parents were involved, too, and follow-up discussions at home ran late into the night and sometimes spilled over into coming weeks.

Our leadership teams, comprised of health professionals, secular and religious teachers, and admired and respected lay persons, were informed, responsible, in tune, and endowed with good humor. They explained anatomy and physiology frankly and accurately and emphasized the humanistic and spiritual aspects. Such a program has certain advantages over home discussions (although these are vital). It is comprehensive where home talk tends to be sporadic. Imagine the reaction if a father announced, "Tonight we begin a series of three two-hour sessions on sexuality." Also, with peers the boy or girl may feel less self-conscious and be cheered to find that he/she isn't all *that* different from others. And some feelings may be more comfortably shared with peers.

But the best of formal courses will not suffice, and many courses are shallow, distorted, and ineptly taught. Only one-third of the nation's schools offer "family life" or "sex education" courses. Sometimes teachers have minimal training and scant native ability and are subjected to outside pressures. Whenever anyone talks to somebody else's kids about sex, steam is a likely by-product. Our church program picked up a few complaints of "Too frank to suit me!"

At home, Jo and I focused on climate rather than code. Recently Jennifer remarked, "I can't recall your ever telling me specifically what I shouldn't do, but I understood your values." Jo and I believe that sexuality—though a special gift—cannot be understood or appreciated apart from our total being, and we aimed at the development of complete, moral, affectionate persons. I feel so strongly that sexual morality must be anchored at the center of our framework of values and cross-braced throughout. I have no enthusiasm for gimmicks. A minister recommended: "Write a pledge to yourself on a piece of paper, fold it, and put it in your pocket or purse. When the going gets heavy, feel the paper for reassurance and courage." I find this a mite shallow and legalistic. I should be able to resist a myriad of temptations without toting around the equivalent of the United States code. I prefer responses grounded in a pervasive attitude of love and respect.

We wanted the children to observe that our marriage was not only caring, but also vibrantly romantic (if not always ecstatic). There's a universal yearning for assurance we are products of love. Maybe we weren't conceived on schedule; perhaps we were an unplanned "caboose"—still we wish to believe we came from a caring union and were wanted and welcome, if after the fact.

A Father Shares

We talked about sex in paired discussions and as a total family. Barbara once remarked to her mother, "I'm glad I can talk as comfortably with daddy as with you." Often our aftersupper discussions centered on a friend's problem, which might also be a shared concern. Somebody else's case history is good discussion material. We also talked about movies.

I keep returning to building a broad context. High school and college counselors report increased sex relations outside marriage. Sometimes this sharing is part of a continuing relationship with mutual investment; again, it is a matter of "hopping into bed." The utter lack of restraint is disturbing, but maybe the implications are more alarming. Counselors say the youngsters are looking for intimacy but frequently they aren't finding it, even in bed—or *especially* in bed. Non-intimate sexual intimacy is creating relationship problems accompanied by anxiety and depression.[1] Like the rest of us, today's young people expect a great deal from their relationships but often aren't willing to invest the necessary time, effort, and patience. Their disappointments and dysfunctions arising from premarital liaisons may spoil their marital relationships. The performance-oriented student ("I make A+ on everything else so why not A+ on sex?") may have difficulty fulfilling either self or spouse.

Help your child (while a toddler, if that's still available to you) to appreciate himself or herself both as a person and as a member of a gender. The nature and dictates of gender are widely discussed. My own view is that males and females aren't as different as we used to think or as similar as some modernists assert. Whichever sex, a child should feel complete and competent, comfortable in who and what he or she happens to be. I believe we must basically be true to ourselves while also remaining attentive to the other person's personality and needs. In our role modeling, we should avoid the extremes of overindulging the child or abandoning him. I used to wince at a mother and son who, in church, couldn't keep their hands off each other. This was more than innocent affection; she took that half-grown boy with her to *her* Sunday school class.

Gender roles are part of our culture, and fathers should model natural and useful "male" characteristics while also showing tenderness and compassion. Dr. Brazelton, the pediatrician and author, says:

> I would cast a firm vote for parents who are different. I have seen the foundering of a child whose parents tried vainly to treat him with a kind of neuter attitude, as if they were one sex instead of two. In the place of compromising with each other, they stifled their individual—and differing—relations to him, thereby blurring the personal honesty and integrity that should be the essence of a child's relationship with each parent.[2]

Perhaps a scripture applies here: "Having gifts that differ, let us use them" (Rom. 12:6).

I wasn't macho—didn't choose to be, couldn't have been. Although my role was reasonably "masculine," I also felt comfortable changing a baby or baking a cake. My boys enjoy their homes—cooking, decorating, entertaining, growing plants. My daughters are good at many activities traditionally associated with males.

I demonstrated my affection for Jo—the children saw that I am fond of her face and figure and that we both like to be cuddled and pampered. My appreciative looks at, and comments about, attractive women gave notice I was alive and well, and they drew sly teasing.

I was "physical" with the children, too, but began backing away somewhat about the time of puberty. There is an inherent awkwardness about adolescence on both sides, and the child's struggle for independence dictates some reduction in hugs and kisses; even so, if I were doing it over, I would strive for a continuum of affectionate contact. Girls complain that fathers become reticent to touch them, but I suspect that there is a sharper separation of fathers and sons. In a *New York Times* essay, Robert J. Christian says that back there somewhere he began giving his sons handshakes instead of hugs, and now he aches for the old embraces. When his boys were babies, he rocked them and kissed them, and he enjoyed it, even at 3 a.m. Now he has only those empty handshakes.[3]

Concerning sexual guidance, I abhor the protectionist approach, which often inculcates fear and shame. It would be an empty victory to shepherd a daughter into marriage still a virgin at the cost of her ability to share freely with her husband. How can we fail to see that we are producing sexual cripples?

Negative approaches are appealingly simple: Don't talk about sex and maybe it will go away. Or, paint a scary picture: "Under the circumstances you'll absolutely abhor the experience. You'll probably get VD or become pregnant (or get the girl pregnant), which is the worst thing that can ever happen to anyone. Besides, you'll carry the shame forever and ruin any chances for a good marriage." Caution is warranted but ought not to be the central theme. Also, I feel that "My daddy would kill me" or "It would kill my mother" aren't the best motivations.

We ought to be honest about our values. For example, I would prefer that my child have premarital sex (even be promiscuous) than be uncaring or mean at his/her core. (Not that there has to be a choice.) I believe we should build understanding and motivation from the inside out. Dr. Erik Erikson, authority on human development, stresses that a young person should establish his own sense of identity before becoming intimate with another.[4] If the youngster has self-esteem and a sense of social responsibility, he will say: "I care enough about myself and others to delay gratification awaiting the right person and the right time."

"Hold on!" some will say. "If I picture sex as good, I'll make it too inviting. And if I tell my children I'll stand behind them no matter what, I'll encourage *what.*" These are real concerns, but are simply risks we must take. I believe that we have to commit ourselves unequivocally to our children. Sometimes the costs are high. Let me tell you about parents who were put to the test.

Susan and Sam (I'll call them) were senior class superlatives but remained unspoiled. Occasional dating turned steady and Sam was practically living at Susan's house. Then, in the summer, they revealed to Susan's parents that she was pregnant.

The parents were shocked, hurt, angry. Their dreams for Susan, including college, collapsed. They had tried to be good parents and had failed. Why had Susan and Sam done this to them? When Susan, looking like the little girl she'd so recently been, fell sobbing into her mother's arms, recrimination yielded to a resolve to bring reason to the unreasonable situation.

Susan and Sam wanted to do what was right and best. The four parents pledged their support but cautioned the two young people that any resolution depended upon their being self-accepting, generous with each other, and industrious.

They married in our chapel with friends and relatives attending. They lived with Susan's parents, then took an economy apartment. Sam worked while attending college, and when the baby was several months old, Susan took a job and the grandmothers baby-sat. Within two years, the young family was fairly self-sufficient. Meanwhile, they had maintained their self-respect, friends, and church relationship.

Whenever I saw Sam and Susan and their little son walking to church—the child looking up lovingly and confidently at his adoring parents—I felt reassured about family values and possibilities. I resolved that if something like this should happen to one of my children, I would muster compassion and help to make the best of the unfortunate situation. (Granted, marriage might not be the answer.) And if I was sincere, why shouldn't I let my children know of my commitment?

When Barbara, and later Jennifer, reached sixteen, I shared something like this: "You will be receiving new privileges, having new adventures, and assuming new responsibilities. Your mother and I are confident you'll do the right thing and we thank you for granting us this sense of security. But if you ever need to talk with us about anything, be assured we will listen. There's no problem we cannot tackle together." For some reason, I didn't communicate this commitment to my sons. (I believe I generally felt less comfortable talking about sexuality with them than with the girls.) Recently, Larry mentioned my talking with the girls. "I knew that what you said applied to me, too, and it made me feel secure."

These are days of early physical maturation and mobility and peer and media enticements. New challenges have been added to the old pressures of passion and desire to please. Such an era demands the strongest, most reliable system of discipline, and I recommend self-respect and regard for others. You will exercise close supervision at the beginning, of course; but you should gradually and regularly relinquish control. After all, you will not be there when feelings rise and someone presses, "If you love me—" or "Everybody's doing it."

NOTES

[1]Ira J. Dreyfuss, "Many in College Troubled by Non-Intimate Intimacy," Associated Press, in *Atlanta Journal*, May 3, 1979, p. 3B.

[2]See Acknowledgments.

[3]Robert J. Christian, "Let Me Hug My Sons as They Grow Older," *New York Times*, June 17, 1979, sec. 4, p. 19.

[4]Some of Erikson's concepts are outlined in "Erik Erikson: The Quest for Identity," Newsweek, Dec. 21, 1970, p. 84, and Robert Coles, "Profiles: The Measure of Man" parts I and II, *The New Yorker*, Nov. 7, 1970, p. 51, and Nov. 14, 1970, p. 59.

Should
My Child
Compete?

_____ **14**

"Hello, Jennifer, how are things going?"

"Fine, dad. I've got a lot to tell you when you get home. Would you believe I'm talking to you upside down?"

"Well, get yourself right-side up and call your mother to the phone. I only have a minute before leaving the hotel."

Jo came on and explained that Jennifer was suspended like an orangutan from an exercise bar fastened in a doorway. "She's excited over the possibility of joining a gymnastics team at the Y."

"Sounds good."

"I hope so, for her sake. But it's an ambitious program for a twelve-year-old. And it sounds expensive!"

Six years later, Jo and I watched Jennifer perform with the varsity gymnastics team of the University of Florida, where she held an athletic scholarship. Behind lay a thousand practice sessions, the sacrificing of competing interests, a few tears, and several minor injuries. The costs for Jo and me: fifteen hundred dollars; a lot of chauffeuring; moments of suspended breathing, and our own weariness from camping on obdurate bleachers.

It was a good investment. During adolescence—usually an awkward period—Jennifer developed strength, stamina, coordination, poise, and self-assurance. She learned that remarkable accomplishments can be achieved step by step, and she became philosophical about winning and losing. She developed a lifetime interest in total health, formed lasting friendships, and expanded her horizons. She won scholarships and later earned money teaching and judging. And gymnastics provided enjoyable recreation.

Millions of youngsters in their preteens and early teens engage in competitive sports, but for the individual parent, "Should my child compete?" remains a tough question in a series: Which sport? Which program? What about injury and emotional pressures? Time, and money?

There are no answers to apply universally, because children and their family situations vary so. Here, for example, are divergent mother's-eye-views of the same sport: "Don't say 'Little League' to me! It reminds me of our lost summer. Billy wasn't keen on playing, had little talent, and spent most of his time on the bench. My two-year-old and I spent eternities on those hard bleachers, which served as a landing spot for my husband between trips to tell the coach how to run his team. Toward the end of the season, Billy took a bad spill and Roy let him quit. All of us were relieved."

Another mother said: "It's great. Our son loves every minute of it; my husband is scorekeeper; and my daughter and I work in the concession booth. This is how we spend our summers, and we love it."

For a child's involvement in a sport to be productive and pleasant, the child's motivations and readiness and the parents' inclinations and resources must be considered. Each child's situation is unlike any other's. Interests, needs, skills, maturity level, and physical condition must be evaluated and matched to the prospective activity. Here are guidelines gathered from a dozen experts and my own experiences.

Motivation. "Important for both emotional and physical reasons," says Fred L. Allman, Jr., Atlanta orthopedic surgeon and a past president of the American College of Sports Medicine. "The reluctant youngster is more likely to be injured. Many boys are pressured into contact sports by their father, buddies, girl friend, or coach. We doctors sometimes see boys who *want* to be injured—it's a socially acceptable way out. Even if X-rays show no fracture, a few boys will beg us to say they have a broken bone. The youngster most likely to find satisfaction in a given sport is the one who plays because he enjoys it—participation complements his image of himself."

Medical. A preparticipation exam by the child's physician can evaluate maturity level and physical condition and minimize risks. If another doctor makes the exam, a complete medical history should be taken. Medical attention should either be immediately available or obtainable through a prearranged plan. Responsibility should be clearly fixed.

Conditioning. Anyone participating in, or planning to participate in, a sport should engage in a year-round conditioning program that takes into account the individual's situation, the sport, and the desired level of proficiency. A good program will improve (a) muscular strength and endurance (through weight lifting and calisthenics), (b) general endurance (jogging, swimming, cycling), and (c) flexibility (rhythmic stretching exercises).

In contact sports, Dr. Allman notes, the majority of serious injuries involve the joints—first the knee, and then the ankle. A youngster with joints that are abnormally loose or tight is especially vulnerable. Evaluation requires a thorough physical examination by a knowledgeable and experienced physician. The muscles are the joint's first line of defense, Dr. Allman notes. If joints are excessively relaxed, the muscles can be strengthened through conditioning. The reverse problem, tightness, can be alleviated through rhythmic stretching exercises. Also of concern are the growing ends of the long bones of the arms and legs. In childhood, these ends, the epiphyses, are separate from the shafts. Until knitting occurs (usually at puberty), they are easily injured.

Reasonably early participation in a favored sport can be a precaution against injury later at the B-team or varsity level, Dr. Allman advises. "With conditioning, the body is wonderfully able to stand stresses, but it cannot take sudden or repeated stresses to which it is not accustomed—something has to give."

Equipment and facilities. Juniors deserve good equipment, particularly protective gear properly fitted, but sometimes get inappropriate hand-me-downs. Generally, playing time, playing area, and equipment should be scaled down from adult proportions.

Matching competitors. Usually done on the basis of grade, age, height, and weight, varying with the sport. But other factors should be considered. Dr. J. Roswell Gallagher, clinical professor of pediatrics,

Yale University School of Medicine, offers the example of the slow-maturing boy of fourteen—chubby, awkward, with little skill, his knees poorly supported, his muscles as yet undeveloped. Such a lad, Gallagher says, will be better matched with younger boys. "Pushy parents who refuse to take maturation into account do their children a disservice." He also contrasts the alert, zestful youngster and the indifferent and lackadaisical one. "Routinely to place a child with those who will not stimulate his interest or yield him the satisfaction or competition that he needs may be more dangerous—and certainly is less rewarding—than placement with older and larger opponents."

Quality of supervision. Rarely does a program rise above the quality of the coaching, officiating, and administration. Concerning coaching, pertinent questions include: Does he (she) like children and understand their growth and development? A good leader knows which activities are appropriate and moves participants through graduated progressions of skill and effort, making adjustments as he "reads" his youngsters.

Is the coach a good disciplinarian? Is he firm, fair, and reasonable—or does he explode and deprecate the offender as a person or pout and sulk? Beware of a leader with personal problems who redirects his hostilities and frustrations at youngsters. And watch for continuing personality conflicts.

Does the coach focus on his own needs—or those of the participants? The coach who features himself a Vince Lombardi putting miniature Green Bay Packers through their paces is a menace. Little people dressed up like, and acting like, big people may be cute, but they are being victimized. Does the coach let weaker players compete, affording them a sense of belonging and contributing? In some leagues and federations, participation is mandated.

Is the coach conversant with established practices and procedures? Is he a good teacher? Does he allow for natural style and creative flair? Is he attentive?

The most authoritative statement on junior sports is one issued by a coalition of health professionals and educators.* The group says that in sports having collision hazards (baseball, basketball, football, ice hockey, soccer, softball, wrestling), the risks are usually associated with the conditions under which play is conducted and the quality of supervision. "Unless a school or community can provide exemplary supervision—medical and educational —it should not undertake competitive sports, especially collision sports, at the preadolescent level," the group declared. Programs should emphasize health and recreational values rather than competitiveness, and interschool athletics should not detract from the total educational experience.

The coalition endorsed competitive sports for the upper, and only upper, elementary grades and listed as examples of appropriate activities archery, bowling, golf, skating, swimming, tennis, and track. Boxing was specifically rejected.[1]

Intensity. What level of proficiency is desirable? As a parent, what degree of commitment will I support?

It's often said that junior sports generate excessive emotional stress. One longtime observer, G. Lawrence Rarick, professor of physical education, University of California, Berkeley, doesn't think this assertion is justified. He notes that "The real

*American Academy of Pediatrics; American Medical Association's Committee on Medical Aspects of Sports; American Association for Health, Physical Education, and Recreation; and Society of State Directors of Health, Physical Education, and Recreation.

threat is in those programs where children are exploited to satisfy the whims of overly ambitious parents, coaches, and community boosters. Programs geared to these motivations can lead to overly long and excessively arduous training sessions, with the tendency to start sports specializations too early."

Programs that push too hard deserve rebuke, but so do the sloppy and undisciplined programs which teach faulty skills, spawn injuries, and cause the boy or girl to lose interest. Dr. Allman comments:

> Discipline is the mainstay of any organized endeavor, whether it's music or athletics. A certain amount of dedication should be expected of the participant. These days, we don't exert ourselves physically without prodding. This is true of an adult exercise class and of ten-year-old swimmers. Just to mature properly, children need some prodding. The important thing is, each kid is different and will react differently. Some thrive on pressure, others on sweet talk.

The coalition mentioned earlier deplored high-pressure contests, including play-offs, bowl contests, and all-star contests; excessive publicity; pep squads; commercial promotions; paid admissions; victory celebrations; elaborate recognition ceremonies; and "exploitation of children in any form."

Parental sins range from overexuberance to gross misconduct. Sometimes (if rarely) fathers turn playing areas into combat zones. They hurl vituperation at coaches, officials, and players. On occasion, there is a fistfight, a stabbing, a shooting. Maybe kids would be better off playing while these obstreperous dads are at work.

It's usually the coach who sets the standards and decides the pace. Few topflight coaches are satisfied with average performance; with anything short of excellence, they feel their talents are underutilized. If practice time and other resources are withheld, they feel thwarted. In our society generally, and in athletics especially, winning is a yardstick of professional achievement. The best approach for the parent, then, is to select a program whose pace seems right for the child. A serious failure of consensus among coach, participant, and parent is like cutting a leg off a three-legged stool.

Jennifer's first coach was ambitious, as were some of the parents. Jo and I weren't sure that a sport should "consume" a twelve-, thirteen-, fourteen-year-old. When practices cut into family sharing, when I felt squeezed financially, when I saw signs of excessive strain—then I felt like shouting, "Hey, there's more to life than uneven bars, floor-ex mat, horse, and beam! Let's relax a bit."

I shared my concerns but tempered them. There were so many conflicting values and imponderables, I wasn't quite sure what it was that I wanted. Jennifer assigned her gymnastics participation a high priority, and I wanted to be supportive. I didn't want to misrepresent her, betray her confidences, violate her rights of privacy, or in any other way jeopardize her standing. Complaints are inherently negative, no matter how they are couched.

My concern intensified when leaders of our parents' club and the coach drafted even more demanding rules for approval by the membership. Practice sessions were mandatory, virtually ruling out extended family vacations. Any gymnast selected to compete in a meet was required to go, even though it might be in Chicago or Miami and as a rule the girl or her family had to pay her way. There would be few exceptions to these rules, we were told.

Because my response reflects some universal concerns, let me share the substance of it:

> We should be deliberate in setting our goals. We can emphasize the development of girls, or we can stress winning and even aspire to produce Olympic class performers. If we believe that a majority of the girls are suited by motivation and potential to become superb gymnasts, perhaps we should gear up for a demanding program. But we ought not misread the girls, who must ultimately be the decision-makers. If we go the high road and the schedule and other pressures are too demanding, what then?
>
> Proficiency is a function of time. The girl, together with her parents, must decide whether gymnastics is worth curtailing school functions, family sharing, and (most important of all) a bit of time to call her own and spend in such way as she may choose. Having already adopted Sunday practices because of limited gym time, I think we've already pushed pretty far.
>
> None of us wants a meandering, do-as-you please program. But how far do we want to go in the other direction? What price do we wish to pay?

The team continued to be highly competitive and ranked well in regional and national meets, but the rules were not enforced as strictly as the guidelines had implied.

Jo and I marveled at Jennifer's perseverance. After competing marginally for several years, she became a regular in her junior year. Then, in her senior year, she elected to switch to her high school team, where the program was more relaxed, and seasonal rather than year-round. This allowed her full participation in senior activities.

As a member of the University of Florida team, Jennifer received a grant equal to her out-of-state tuition, and in her sophomore year, she received full tuition. But after two years, she decided not to return to the team, as the satisfaction derived in the gym was no longer commensurate with the demands. She felt the need to devote more time to other aspects of college life.

I deeply appreciate those who contributed so much to Jennifer. Because she was bright and well-rounded, her academics remained high and she rarely showed excessive stress. Her participation was expensive, but she herself sold six thousand candy bars at a dime apiece to fellow high school students to buy airline tickets. Jo and I enjoyed local meets and a few out-of-town ones, and I believe we were generally understanding and supportive.

But if I faced the same dilemma again, I would have the same qualms. Again, "Are the rewards commensurate with the demands?" would defy a neat, conclusive answer.

Let me share some of my impressions about sports:

Don't arbitrarily impose your values upon your child. Let him sample a variety of sports, then choose one or more to suit his interests, capabilities, and opportunities. Although versatility is desirable, most of us like to excel in at least one field.

Safety is important, but it isn't the only factor. (Bowling isn't for everybody.) My own parental preference would be a relatively safe sport that enhances total body fitness (examples: swimming and running) over a sport with a relatively high chance of injuries that may impose chronic limitations for the rest of one's life (example: football). If my child strongly preferred football, I would insist on the precautions and safeguards I've described. I would also encourage his participation, additionally , in a lifetime sport of his choice. Be sensitive to your child's temperament. Some kids thrive on spirited competition and physical confrontation, others abhor such activities. Not every child will relish having a coach slap him on the rump and bellow, "Go get 'em, tiger!"

If there's a get-acquainted meeting for parents, be there. Join a parents' club if there is one; if there isn't, help to organize one. It can be a communications channel, a sounding board, a supportive arm, and a vehicle for soliciting community support.

When appropriate, share information and ideas with the coach. Don't assume an adversary role, which will undermine your child's respect for coaches and officials. Avoid imposing on the coach's professionalism.

Inform yourself about the sport; you will increase your enjoyment, and you may be able to help your child.

Watch for signs of fatigue and injury; don't let problems slide—get a professional opinion. Also, watch for changes in temperament (unaccustomed flaring, argumentativeness, crying, withdrawal). If things go sour, allow the child room to work things out before you intercede. Don't yank him out of a program precipitately; on the other hand, don't force him to continue over his persistent protests. If he is in a no-go situation, guide him into another sport or program.

Think through your serious concerns (academics, money, etc.) and then discuss them forthrightly with your child. Don't be capricious; offer solutions or options. Don't let misgivings fester and undermine your relationship with your child and mar his participation.

The average youngster spends a lot of time in sports activities, the serious contender a huge hunk of his or her life. A serious swimmer may spend as much time in that blue, wet "other" world as in the classroom. Such investment deserves evaluation. Slack off—or try harder? How can other interests be accommodated?

Dr. Gallagher, the Yale pediatrics professor, gives sports a high score for exercise, recreation, learning to win and lose, and companionship:

> They are a boon to those who have been unable to achieve success and satisfaction—and the self-esteem these yield—from any other source. It is in the competitive atmosphere of sports that the civilized child is exposed to stimuli closely approximating the fight for survival. Learning how to react appropriately is an indispensable part of strong, versatile character development. Besides, with or without parental approval, most children are going to compete in sports of some kind (sandlot or whatever), which is added reason for sanctioning well-supervised activities.

The first time I saw Jennifer compete in college gymnastics, I was aware of a new dimension of grace and poise. A companion, who is knowledgeable in the sport, pinpointed the difference: "She is holding her chin up. That's something you cannot be taught; you have to feel that way about yourself." This may be the ultimate test: the sport should complement the youngster's image of himself, as Dr. Allman said. I hope that participation in an appropriate sport will help your child to hold his chin up throughout his life.

NOTE

[1]"Competitive Athletics for Children of Elementary School Age," *Pediatrics*, Oct. 1968, p. 703.

Traditions
to Treasure

_____ **15**

The first squabble that Jo and I had was over a Christmas tree—she paid too much for it, or so I asserted. Strange. It was _her_ money and we'd just begun dating. (Apparently this confession isn't sufficient penitence. Reading over my shoulder just now, Jo goaded, "You really were ugly!")

I'm glad Jo is sentimental. I'm saddened when someone says, "At our house, we don't make a fuss over birthdays, holidays, and the like." I know what that family is missing, because in my childhood home special occasions weren't very special. That's why Jo and I had that argument. I was following a script: "Don't invest too heavily in a holiday or you'll be disappointed."

At Christmas, my parents' temperaments clashed. _Things_ weren't important to dad, and although he managed exclamations of surprise over his gifts, he promptly squirreled them away. If, later, my brother or I mentioned the need of a belt or handkerchief, dad went to his cache and fished one out. So, I chose dad's gifts to suit my own tastes as well as his.

Dad's preoccupation with his newspaper shop conspired with his disdain for festivity to keep him out of the shopping arena until store-closing time Christmas Eve. At best, he wasn't a discriminating shopper, and with stocks depleted—well, his gifts for mother fell short of her standards of elegance, and she told him so.

Mother selected my gifts, usually inexpensive but special. Trouble was, she held the anticipated presents over my head to keep me in line, and by Christmas there would have been many revocations and reinstatements. I got the impression Christmas depended more on performance than love.

The tempestuous nature of our household at Christmas and throughout the year rendered me susceptible to "holiday syndrome." Anniversaries encourage summing up, and I used to brood over failed opportunities and be apprehensive while, all around me, people seemed mirthful. Jo and the children are powerful antidotes.

Jo's family was frugal, but her mother could always lay hands on "milk and egg" money. They had happy times together. With this heritage, Jo insisted that holidays and birthdays be special times.

When the children were young, I set aside a day for shopping in our favorite department store. While the kids bought presents at the Secret Shop, which catered to children, Jo and I bought their gifts. We regrouped into appropriately exclusive bands to complete our purchases. We lunched in the store's cafeteria and rode the "Pink Pig" monorail train. At home, I baked loaves of banana bread, and we went out as a family to deliver them. I remember a serenade for our pediatrician with a high-pitched voice demanding "piggy" pudding instead of the figgy kind. We also went caroling.

On Christmas Eve we had with us my mother and father, friends and neighbors (mostly childless folk and always including a Jewish friend who was a skilled elf). I got home from the paper at ten for snacks and conversation. Then, with the children in bed, we assembled toys and tested them—sometimes too vigorously. Jo and I would stumble to bed at two, and the alarm in Randy's head would go off at five.

Now there are fourteen of us, including my brother, Jimmy, who is a teacher here in Atlanta; his wife, Liz; and their son, Tom. On Christmas Eve, we attend a candlelight service at our church and reassemble at our house for turkey dinner. At the table, Jo expresses appreciation for our family, then lights a candle and passes it to the person on her right with "Merry Christmas, Randy (or whoever)," and the candle and greeting move around the circle.

We are geared to the least among us. For several years, we have gathered on Christmas morning for Santa Claus at the home of grandsons Jake and Jody, and next year we will go to Amy's house. With such a crowd, we discussed drawing names but decided instead to cut expenses, and many gifts are handcrafted. Most seasons we also have a brunch with Jimmy, Liz, and Tom and a party at Randy's.

At Thanksgiving it's turkey time again. With grandchildren, I plan to reinstate a longtime custom. In advance, we cut out magazine illustrations representative of autumn, harvest, family, and other blessings, and pasted these on cardboard. On the back, we wrote an appropriate Bible verse. At the table, each person had a card, displayed the picture, and read aloud the verse.

We used to celebrate all holidays, and even the visit of the Tooth Fairy. Easter meant dainty frocks, finished at midnight, and little-man suits gladly worn to church. The bunny filled waiting baskets with candy eggs, and we hunted for real eggs which had stubbornly refused dye. On the Fourth of July we flew the flag and cooked out. On New Year's Eve we banged on cooking pans, and the next day indulged superstition and ate black-eyed peas. On Halloween we traipsed through the neighborhood harvesting treats.

My parents ignored their birthdays, but I publicized mine. I had one party, given by an aunt while mother was ill. I embarrassed her by running up the block yelling, "What did 'ya bring me?" What they brought me were marbles, tops, ball-bouncing paddles, five dime yo-yos and a deluxe twenty-five-cent model that hummed. My aunt, having only daughters, consulted a party book for boy-sounding games, but the lads rejected these and engaged in their own favorite sport—mayhem. Parties are important to children; few other experiences are so vividly remembered.

Today, we have cake and ice cream—except Jimmy and I prefer candle-lit banana pudding. We sing and the birthday person makes a wish, blows out the candles, and opens the gifts. Somewhere along the line, we dropped "Pin the Tail on the Donkey."

Years ago, on warm spring nights our street resounded with the cries of neighborhood children at play. I helped them catch lightning bugs, which magically transformed mayonnaise jars into flashing lanterns. If mother was visiting us, she organized games of "Ain't No Boogers Out Tonight" and regaled the youngsters with tales from her childhood—how she and her brothers and sisters startled passers-by with make-believe snakes. Parents clustered and socialized—another lost pleasure.

We've kept alive a tradition of "private" jokes—pithy sayings that convey an implied message. I judge a family to be close when it has a large repertory of intramural quips. Some Bugg-isms are:

"Don't be a martyr." Because my mother would forgo pleasures but remind us of the sacrifice, I ordered the children: "If you want something, speak up or forever hold your peace," and so a remaining slice of pie might be divided into six forkfuls. Abnegation still brings a chorus of "Don't be a martyr."

"Okay, Aunt Pearl!" My maiden aunt would let conversation slip by, then become interested and ask for a replay. Anyone doing that is chided, "Okay, Aunt Pearl!"

"Look up here! Look down there!" announces breathtaking scenery. It originated when Jo tried to call my attention to natural wonders while I struggled to keep the car on hairpin curves in North Carolina mountains.

Our traditions have persisted in spite of maturation, competing schedules, and dispersion. They're fun and require no justification, but I'd like to lift up some values.

When we intentionally come together, we demonstrate our interdependence and unity. Each person has a special place in the family circle, and the family in turn, is a unit in larger associations—community, nations, or church. We stand for something! The extended family provides children with guidance, direction, and a sense of belonging.

We learn to give generously and receive graciously.

Symbolism and ritual tap our creativity, and we share feelings and values that we cannot articulate. In a day of technological wonders, a microwave oven lacks the magic of the glow of a shared fire or the warmth of clasped hands. In a time of furious change, primitive feelings and connections remain the same.

We celebrate the continuity of our lives. We *can* go home again, if only in our thoughts. Getting in touch with our roots gives us stability; shared expectations lend direction and purpose.

Something that grips us—demands of us—is laden with emotion—deserves review. Here are some considerations:

Accept hybridization. Brides and grooms bring into marriage chauvinistic prejudices and wariness befitting United Nations debates. "*Rhubarb* pie for Thanksgiving? You gotta be kidding!" To adopt outright another family's customs is like transplanting a grown tree—better to plant your own and bud and graft from old stock.

Don't imprison yourself. Family traditions are great, and even family skeletons are okay, but don't lock yourself in the closet with them. One family spent its Christmases at its mountain cottage but secretly hated it. When someone let his discontent show, negative feelings gushed out. Next Christmas they stayed home. We tried Thanksgiving in a restaurant. The kids chorused, "Let's not do this again!" In contrast, we spent a Thanksgiving camping in Florida in eighty-degree weather and liked it.

If a tradition becomes sacrosanct, thoughts of being absent can be intimidating. When Randy spent Christmas holidays skiing in Switzerland, we missed him terribly but lived up to our resolve not to make either ourselves or him miserable.

Pace yourself. Be realistic in your expectations;

guard against physical and mental fatigue; resist impulses toward profligate spending. Overextension and overexertion can cause you to feel victimized and bereft.

Capture spirituality, but don't be a demon about it. I cherish the religious and get peeved at the secular—let the clothiers *have* Easter and the credit-card companies Christmas! But I'm as intolerable bah-humbugging materialism as I'd be scrooging the true Christmas spirit. Come to think of it, I miss the repetitive musical sagas of Rudolph the red-nosed reindeer and Alvin the chattering chipmunk.

The Rev. Robert Farrar Capon, Episcopalian priest and an author, says we won't "Put Christ Back in Christmas" (as bumper stickers implore) by being archly indignant of "White Christmas" and "Home for the Holidays." The incarnation isn't so much about stars and angels as about babies and families. In a *Redbook* essay, Father Capon says:

> I commend to you a relaxed conscience about your Christmas festivities. . . . Go to it with a glad good will. Make this your earthiest Christmas yet. As much as you can, throw out the fake materialities and the snooty spiritualities and dig your heels into the real ground of faith—into the humanity that God in the manger holds up as the final revelation of himself and into all the delectabilities of the world that man, in Christ, was meant to love.[1]

Here's a miscellany of suggestions for family traditions:

• Prepare Advent candles and share a lighting service on each of the four Sundays of Advent and finally on Christmas Eve or Christmas Day.

• During the Christmas holidays, make things together; decorations cut from flour-and-salt dough and baked; gleaming hard candies of assorted artificial flavors and in varied cake-coloring hues; gingerbread boys and girls (and don't forget to share with Santa); divinity candy and chocolate fudge; strings of popcorn and cranberries; candles; personalized stockings to be "hung by the chimney with care"; and gifts, of course.

• In lieu of Christmas cards, send out a newsy letter.

• Make valentines. My children expect my traditional gift, a chocolate bar.

• On birthdays, anniversaries, Mother's Day, and at other times, write personalized letters of appreciation to your spouse and children.

• Seize upon "instant" traditions. Television personality Harry Reasoner and his children went to a friend's farm, floundered through snow, cut a Christmas tree, and hauled it home. The next year, someone asked Reasoner's eight-year-old daughter if the family had bought their tree. "Oh, no," she said, "we always go to the Whites and cut our tree."[2]

• Widen your circle at Thanksgiving and Christmas and through the year. Invite lonely and disadvantaged persons, college students, and foreign visitors to share your gatherings. Join other families. We used to drop in on friends Sunday afternoons, an enjoyable practice that isn't done much anymore.

• Draw from other cultures. Through Jewish neighbors and a mixed school constituency, we have learned about the Judaic side of our Judeo-Christian heritage.

• Sing together while traveling or when gathered round the piano.

• Hang hand-lettered banners and posters that say "Welcome Home!" or "Congratulations!"

• Together, visit the old homeplaces; chat with the matriarchs and patriarchs and collect oral histories. Photocopy historical materials and distribute them. Hold family reunions.

• Enjoy mementoes. Let your son have grandfather's watch now, your daughter wear grandmother's ring. Label heirlooms and photographs before their history is lost. Get those jumbled and crimped photographs into albums.

• Record family events on film or tape.

• Prepare a "This Is Your Life" scrapbook for each child. Include art, writings, clippings, etc. Color copying can be done at modest prices.

• Establish a nook for special-interest displays. Our living room shelves exhibit seashore collections.

• Together, watch special events on television. We mourned the death of John F. Kennedy and celebrated the astronauts' successes.

• Invite young relatives to spend the night with you, and do special things. At my house, I cook pancakes, and eating contests ensue. Visiting my brother, my kids enjoyed "wild" things like watergun battles.

Childhood happiness and security seem inalienable rights, and traditions enhance these feelings. Not only are traditions enjoyed at the moment; they may also be put in the "bank." Sir James Barrie wrote: "God gives us memory so that we may have roses in December." One of the finest gifts of parenthood is to provide these experiences and equip the child with the necessary motivation and resources for establishing and relishing customs of his own design.

Willa Cather said of childhood recollections, "There are those memories. One cannot get another set; one has only those." I would issue a mild objection: You have only one crack at child*hood* memories, but child*like* memories continue to be available. Thanks to Jo and the children, I have enjoyed a second childhood. My grandchildren may usher me into a third. I'm glad my wife is sentimental.

NOTES

[1]Robert Capon, "Let Us Exalt Earth, Not Heaven," *Redbook*, Dec. 1970, p. 62.
[2]Harry Reasoner, "Playing Together, Staying Together, and All That," magazine article.

The
Bittersweet Part:
Letting Go

_____ **16**

Jennifer, our last, has departed to tour Europe, *alone*. She didn't ask me if she could go. Is that because she recently turned twenty-three?

After taking a degree in psychology a year ago, she worked in a restaurant to earn money for graduate school, but a compulsion to see Europe won out, and education will wait. She will be away five months, and already we miss her very much.

All four have left home. It seems they left precipitately; actually, the leave-taking started three decades ago, when Barbara was only two and the others were still twinkles in their parents' eyes.

Jo and I had taken Barbara to a park, and I became aware of "I'm-a-big-girl-now" feelings stirring within her. Clamping her eyes shut, she bravely allowed a monstrous goose to gobble bread out of her palm. And then she insisted that we ride the miniature train, pulled by a steam locomotive. As we stood in line, she demanded, "I want to ride all by myself!"

Reluctantly, I put her aboard. Every time she came around, her intense expression softened into a brave little smile and she let go her grip long enough to wave to us. We let go our feelings long enough to shed some tears.

"Mama," I said, clutching Jo's hand, "your little girl is growing up."

That was one jump in a progression of leaps toward independence. "No, I want to wear *that* dress!" "I can spank my doll if I want to!" "I don't wanta go home now!"

In a flash, it seemed, we found ourselves at the school. Pressing through a crush of humanity, we searched out the door with the assigned teacher's name on it, led her up to the desk, and said, "This is Barbara Bugg." We wanted to add that she got sore throats easily, didn't like spinach, and minded rather well without a lot of shouting. I wanted to sit in the back a while and see if she remained happy. Instead, we turned and walked out.

Now our daughter began assimilating grown-up tools for assertion. I was proud when she stood her ground against a grumpy woman who tried to shoo her and other children from a playground intended for all tenants in our apartment complex. "It's a free country!" Barbara declared, and she continued to swing.

Soon she joined Brownies and donned the sweet little dress and darling cap, round like her face. I took the "official" photograph of the troop, and as Jo and I admired a print, I said, "Wouldn't it be nice if they could stay like this forever?" But they didn't. The camera had stopped the action for only one-fiftieth of a second.

Growing experiences—*separating* experiences:

junior choir, ballet, piano lessons, church camp, Girl Scout camp, joining the church, baby-sitting, slumber parties, Methodist Youth Fellowship. Ballroom dancing classes came, and boyfriends weren't far behind. The first lad who called was so well-scrubbed I doubted he would ever again be comfortable. She seemed sophisticated at times, but at her first dinner party the guests alternated playing records with playing touch football. I found this inconstancy consoling. Tri-Hi-Y, Senior Scouts, writing for the school paper, serving as a counselor-in-training at camp, summer romances.

Boys were calling regularly. If Barbara wasn't home, they sat and chatted with Jo and me. Because they didn't appear serious, I didn't give them a critical eye. But then her crowd began getting driver's licenses, and I lay awake listening for a car to stop and a key to turn in the front door.

In her senior year, I was less essential than before, although there remained a few things I could do: tell Bill when she would be home; lend her a dollar until she could collect for baby-sitting, help plan a program; get up firewood for a hayride. And then I turned around and glimpsed her marching down the aisle in gown and mortarboard—poised, pretty, and mature.

The summer rushed by and I found myself helping load the car with the clothes rack, plastic "sand" bucket filled with toilet articles, versatile popcorn popper. As she got into the car, I handed her some stamps. "Be sure to write," I said, giving her a hug and a kiss. As she and Jo drove away, I asked myself: Is it possible eighteen years have whisked by since I paced that hospital corridor?

Because I had visited the campus earlier, I stayed home to work on a pressing assignment, but I couldn't focus on it. For catharsis, I typed out a sketch describing my bittersweet feelings.

When Jo returned, she reported Barbara was happily situated. "How did your day go?"

"Well, I felt sorta low, but then I wrote—"

"An article about Barbara going away to school!"

"Right. I called it 'Barbara Left Long Ago.' And you know how it ends? *Why did I let her ride that little train?*"

* * *

We don't realize that when the little one shoves his plate away and indignantly fans the air with protesting hands, he's waving goodbye to us. Being unaware is mostly good, although in vexing moments we might be consoled by the assurance that *this*, too, will pass.

The relentless march toward being one's own person accelerates in that notorious period called adolescence, a time when it is no longer appropriate to think like a child or act like a child. Old attachments must be severed or modified, old value systems restructured, new allies and new resources appropriated. If these issues are not resolved by twenty, they will fester and cause trouble at forty.

It's good that youngsters insist on flying solo, for although we parents may grow weary of so many birds cluttering the nest, we don't think it right for a parent to kick out his own child. Yet, as Margaret Meade observed, "The ideal family is one in which parents and children cooperate in bringing their existence to a timely end."[1] Some families fail miserably. They either split in permanent estrangement or fail to complete the transition into interdependence.

Our pediatrician said, "I don't see how a family survives having a thirteen-year-old girl in the house." The best way to survive is to recognize the necessity for the strivings of the adolescent period.

Randy was the epitome of the good, dependable child. (I have become aware that he proceeds through this book quietly and confidently, just as he did in our lives together.) He was serious-minded, but he could also be fun—he laughed at the antics of Lucille Ball and the hijinks of his grandmother. He made A's mostly, and he was just as adept at packing our camping trailer. He was inclined to keep his own counsel, and yet he shared his opinions and feelings with us.

When Randy turned sixteen, we became aware of a change. He seemed quiet, even withdrawn. He was extremely active at school, but even when he was home, he rarely joined in our family conversations. Had we done something to alienate him? Had he decided we weren't good parents? Did a personal problem have him down? We shared our dismay, but Randy denied that anything was wrong: "It isn't complicated. I just don't have much to say—when I do, I'll say it. In the meantime, stop worrying about me."

But we didn't stop worrying; indeed, for a couple of years we were as concerned over Randy's sober aloofness as we were Larry's happy-go-lucky indifference to studies and chores.

Randy entered Emory University, and although the campus is only five minutes away, Jo and I resolved to let him have an "away-from-home" experience. Perhaps it was seeing our willingness to let him be independent that caused him to soften; at any rate, one rainy afternoon he called to see if Jo could run him over to his job at the health center. Then he thought it would be nice if our once-a-week maid did his shirts. On weekends, he borrowed a car, and on Sunday nights we delivered him back to the campus, a shuttle that afforded us brief, but delicious, periods of sharing. Soon he was bringing a friend home for dinner. Then he and his dormitory roommate moved into our garage apartment and shared our evening meal. The last remnant of distance between us was closed during six months' active military duty. I suspect that being away heightened Randy's awareness of how much home and family meant to him.

Now we are close. Recently, Randy said, "Mom, you and dad move the furniture out of the dining room. Monday, I begin a week's vacation and I'm going to spend it painting the dining room and living room." Another time, Jo came in to find a new, deluxe refrigerator in her kitchen, a gift from Randy. These aren't standards by which affection is measured but they are nonetheless tokens of love.

This happy ending moves me to say to parents who are experiencing fallout from a child's growing pains, "Hang in there!" Here are other suggestions:

• When your child is two, prepare him for the responsibilities he will assume at twenty. Gradually allow options—what he will wear, what you will do together, how he will spend money. Expect him to care for some of his things. Add freedoms gradually—some kids move too fast and are overwhelmed, or they usurp control of the family's decision-making mechanism.

• Don't saddle a child with restrictions simply because they applied to an older sibling at the same age. Although you want to avoid rank favoritism, it isn't practical or desirable to balance privileges and gifts precisely. Give heed to individual needs and responsibleness and do any balancing over the long haul.

• Evaluate how you're doing, but don't bog down in continuous appraisal. Dr. Urie Bronfenbrenner, Cornell psychologist, shares: "I would say to parents, number one, that young people do not think as ill of you as you think. Two, that they think you think worse of them than you do. And three, it is not your fault. The nature of the problem is the way life is organized for us."[2]

We don't deserve all the credit—or blame. In spite of severe social deprivation, a class of children that social scientists call "the invincibles" thrive, and for reasons that are not altogether clear.[3] In contrast, some children who are reared in good environments go bad. An interesting case is Patricia Krenwinkel. From her father's report, she enjoyed a better than average childhood. She was gentle and loved animals, belonged to the Camp Fire Girls, sang in church choirs, and attended summer Bible school. But one day while she was nineteen and employed by an insurance company, she skipped out with a guy named Charlie Manson, whose "family" made bloody history.[4]

• Recognize that you will always be partly parent as well as friend. Because your child has typed you as parent, your casual question or comment (such as a roommate might share with impugnity) may be interpreted as an intrusion or imposition.

Recognize that you and your child don't have to agree on issues or even picture your relationship the same way. Maintain mutual respect and you can find unity in disagreements. Say, your child complains that you are too directive, even hovering, but you don't feel you are. Even if you discuss the issue in a friendly and polite way but fail to reconcile your positions, don't feel hurt or diminished; instead, celebrate the fact that you and your child have a mutual investment that allows you to discuss amicably so delicate a matter as your feelings about your relationship. Have something constructive come out of your conversation: "I'm going to back off and give you more room, but remember that I don't love you any less or have any less concern."

• Eventually, you must release the youngster. Instead of going on vacation with the family, Barbara, then a junior in high school, wanted to work in a camp. Jo was distressed at the thought of forfeiting our "last" vacation together. "Let her go her way," I said. "You've been mama to her for sixteen years, and this is the end of the line." We went to our favorite island; Barbara worked. I'm happy to report that we've had vacations together since then.

• When your kids grow up and leave, be sure to send privileges and accountability with them. Some colleges ask parents of dormitory residents (girls, especially) to specify what privileges will be granted. Full privileges, I always said. I didn't expect the college to be a babysitter—besides, I don't think they do that job effectively. I also favor giving the youngster credit cards and letting him pick his own courses of study, but these privileges are conditioned on prior exercising of responsibilities and a fair show of success.

• I believe that beginning at age three or four, a child should receive an allowance—not a stipend contingent on behavior, but a sharing of the family's resources. Our kids began with a quarter, of which fifteen cents was for unrestricted spending and ten cents for savings. The amount topped out at several dollars for teenagers. (That was back in the days of "good" dollars.) The children were allowed to earn money but weren't paid for ordinary household chores like washing dishes, mowing grass, or baby-sitting. Even as youngsters, they had savings accounts, and in the senior year of high school, checking accounts.

My children couldn't keep up with the affluent Jones kids of our community, and they were appreciative of money and judicious in spending it. Jennifer, our champion money manager, could squeeze a dime in her hot little hand even as Larry slurped an ice-cream cone beside her. She had money to lend, often at interest.

Frugality was a way of life. We scraped up money

for camp (ordinarily the children themselves paid half) and even for orthodontia, but our everyday climate was economical. Jo made clothes (even topcoats) for herself and the girls; they had a great tailored look because they were stitched with love. She stayed home with the children when they were little; and when she held outside jobs she arranged to be home when they arrived from school. (For a number of years, she worked with me.) The children were generally generous toward, and supportive of, one another. Now we laugh about the return trips from vacation when we had to pool our coins for our last hamburger stop. Two of the children went to private colleges, one went to a state university, and one to an out-of-state school. Three earned scholarships and all of them worked.

• Discourage grown children from coming back home to live except through necessity or as an interim convenience. After leaving college, Barbara lived with us while she saved money to establish herself in an apartment. She intended to stay a short time; nevertheless, I suggested, ''Let's not let 'one big, happy family' stretch too far. I have seen too many unmarried folk who got that way living with their folks.'' Returning home has two hazards: either the two generations aren't comfortable with each other, or they're *too* comfortable.

• Little boys go out and scrap with their buddies, then come in to touch base and say ''Hi'' before venturing out again. Older children, too, feel a need to come home again, and often they're more appreciative than before, having observed other families and some persons who have no family. Give them latitude to come and go; that way, you will see them more often and derive more enjoyment from their visits.

• Approach the growing-up years as opportunity rather than hazardous duty. Psychologist Alice

Ginott says that teenagers are given a "second chance." They seem so disorganized because they are in the process of reorganizing themselves. "We, as parents, can influence the direction," Dr. Ginott counsels. "How we talk to them can make the difference."[5]

NOTES

[1]Mead, "Can the Family Survive?" *Redbook*, Sept. 1970, p. 52.

[2]"Somebody—Let It, Please God, Be Somebody," *Time*, Dec. 28, 1970, p. 37.

[3]Maya Pines, "Superkids," *Psychology Today*, Jan. 1979, p. 53.

[4]"Trials: Life with Father," *Time*, Feb. 15, 1971, p. 23.

[5]Alice Ginott, "How To Drive Your Child Sane," *Ladies' Home Journal*, Aug. 1977, p. 48.

Who Said "Empty Nest"?

_____ **17**

This past winter, we lost an old friend—our ancient, stoker-fired furnace. "Good riddance!" I said, thinking about the nightly ritual of shoveling coal and extracting clinkers. I handled those chores first, then Randy, then Larry, and back to me again. Man and boy, we wrestled that monster twenty-four years.

The new gas-fired boiler requires only three minutes a week, and I should be ecstatic. Instead, I feel vaguely uneasy. I'm conditioned to believe that warmth must be earned: you cut wood or shovel coal. When I suffer a lapse of memory and head down to placate "Old Fateful" and then remember it's no longer there, I feel slightly bereft.

That's how it has been since the children departed. For three decades, they were at the center of my life. I looked forward to liberation, but now that it has come, I resist it. I miss the activity and sounds of a large and active family, but there are deeper implications. I am aware I'm not as young— or as needed—as I once was.

I don't feel old, but occasionally I'm reminded of my fifty-seven winters. We were brainstorming ideas for church programs and someone suggested "The Aging Parent." What did I think?

"It's a good subject," I allowed, "although Jo and I aren't directly interested inasmuch as our parents are dead."

"Ralph," a sweet young thing chided, "you *are* the aging parent."

I'm still needed, but not so often or as acutely. I can sit down and read the evening paper through where, once, there would be several interruptions: Barbara thrusting a disabled doll at me and confidently ordering, "Sits it, daddy." Or Larry fetching me to get his baseball out of a gutter.

The children have problems, but both the children and their troubles have changed. Now most of the problems are sticky and complicated and ill-suited to intervention. I ache to make things right and kiss away the hurt, as I once did, but I cannot barge in—and what could I do except say "I love you" and "I'm sorry"?

I bump into artifacts. A stringless archery bow tumbles from the hall closet; a storage box in the garage leaks Parcheesi men and Monopoly houses and hotels; Randy's upright piano, which he played with verve, dominates our living room.

But when I pass those two upstairs bedrooms, I miss the children most. The "boys' room" was quickly appropriated for a studio. And since Barbara has been gone more than a decade, few traces of her remain in the other room. But a lot of *Jennifer* lingers: frilly curtains; pastel posters that speak of love and friendship; gymnastics trophies; and a

A Father Shares

menagerie of cats, owls, and frogs. I'll never grow accustomed to saying "guest room." And I suspect we have preserved the decor in order to protect sentiment. We miss those four wonderful people who no longer live with us.

But there are compensations. Being a part-time parent allows me to be a full-time husband. Our new freedom approaches abandon. We can eat a chili dog at five—or a fancy meal with candles at eight. When we go out, there's no baby-sitter to hurry home and relieve. Vacation? Jab a finger at the calendar. Romantic interlude? At the drop of a window shade.

Jennifer doesn't scream, "La-r-r-y-y!" and I don't scream, "Come home this instant!" I can plunge onward toward the secret of a mystery instead of rereading "Peter Rabbit" long after the outcome had become clear. I don't indemnify neighbors for broken glass, wait for the phone, or mop up after a parade of thirsty ball players.

We've been fortunate to have our children remain in metropolitan Atlanta (although we're reconciled to knowing this proximity may not last). Being nearby permits limitless phone calls and frequent visits, including our more elaborate get-togethers on holidays and birthdays. On these occasions, I view our clan gathered round our extended table and feel a pride described in *McCall's* by Otto Friedrich, whose grandmother presided over a tribe of more than one hundred: "As I reflect upon the various goals that we hold up for ourselves and our children . . . to win a seat in the United States Senate, or on the New York Stock Exchange, or to make $100,000 a year at some numbing executive job, or even to be the world's most distinguished brain surgeon—none of them impresses me, as a goal, as any more desirable [than having a large family]."[1]

I am immensely proud of my family—prouder

than I could ever be of a career accomplishment. I will never be a famous writer, but Jake and Jody think I am the world's best storyteller. When their rollicking laughter subsides, their appreciative little eyes survey me. "Granddaddy, you're funny!" Eat your hearts out, William Styron and Joseph Heller!

Although I'm proud of my family, I feel a great debt to a host of relatives and friends—adults who were like a father or mother, and young people slightly older than our own who served as confidants and role models. Grandparents, aunts, uncles, neighbors, church professionals and lay people, pediatricians, dentists, teachers, counselors, and mentors on the job. Example: the scoutmaster who, because I worked nights, took my sons to meetings, risked his life sampling their cooking, and startled Larry—candidate for the pet merit badge—by directing him to have his fish do their tricks.

We enjoyed an extended family of helpers, and one of my duties and privileges was to direct my children into the care of people who had rich gifts and were willing to share them.

Instead of losing four children, we have gained an additional two, plus three grandchildren. Barbara's Harold is big, powerful, intelligent, industrious, generous, and affectionate, a good husband, father, son. He likes camping, fishing, and his mother-in-law. He and I like the same things!

Larry and Flo married young, although after a prolonged courtship. Both sets of parents were keenly aware of the statistical risks but optimistic and supportive. Flo's seriousness of purpose, together with her willingness to get out and enjoy outdoor activities with Larry, has been good for him. Last Mother's Day I wrote this note to her:

Thank you for bringing Amy into our lives; for being a caring mother to her, a good wife to Larry,

A Father Shares

and a loving daughter to Jo and me. Fathers expect closeness with their children-by-birth but can only hope for closeness with children-by-marriage, and I am blessed in this respect—it's easy for me to get misty-eyed thinking about the relationship we enjoy. So have a happy Mother's Day secure in the knowledge you're a good mother and wife, and a wonderful daughter to your long-time parents and us come-latelys.

Being a grandparent is, of course, a delight. After all those years dutifully saying no, I can say yes.

Once when we were camping, Jody ran up and asked, "Granddaddy, you got any money?" I fished out several coins for him, and he scampered away. No demand for accountability. Nice.

Some parents never let their children forget "all we did for you," but I feel in debt of my children. Thanks to them and to Jo, I can allow myself to love and be loved. They have willingly accepted love in lieu of cash. They knew the capricious nature of free-lancing, yet they wanted me to leave the paper, where I had become unhappy. Some fathers complain that their family interferes with their career; I am more capable and better motivated as a writer because of my wife and children.

The children's generosity continues. Sometimes Jo and I have difficulty graciously accepting the reversal of roles. The gang wanted us to enjoy a vacation on our favorite island, Ocracoke, but we said we couldn't afford it.

"Mom," Harold said, "we have found out what you earn on your job, and we're going to hire you to go on vacation."

"And I'm paying for your gasoline," Jennifer added.

We were overwhelmed, as we were when we received this letter from Barbara:

Who Said *"Empty* Nest"?

Dear Mother and Daddy,

I just want to stop a moment and say I love you and think a child is mighty lucky to have had the two of you as parents.

Thank you for always loving me for what I am, including my faults as well as good points. Thank you for always being honest with me in your feelings. Thank you for the many moments in my growing when I haven't quite succeeded, but you never let me feel as though I had failed—even though sometimes it was at your expense. Thank you for letting me become independent, and for showing me the importance of responsibility. Thanks for the things you gave me when it meant that you did without. Most of all, thank you for always being there when I needed you—and for giving me life.

If I accomplish nothing else as a mother, I hope my children will grow up feeling as loved as I always have. I hope they know how wonderful the closeness of a whole family can be—one filled with love and affection for one another; one that enjoys doing things together; one that shares the hardships together and grows from these experiences; one that always has an open door for talking about anything freely; and one that feels the importance of sharing.

So, if I sometimes forget to say out loud what I feel, know that I've always been proud to be your daughter, and I love you both dearly.

BARBARA

Celebrate being a father! Open your arms and your heart to your children. Let them know—by the way you look at them, talk with them, relate to them—you are glad you have them and are proud they are like you and try to pattern after you.

Don't swap your opportunities to be together for other achievements and satisfactions, real or empty. Give yourself to your family and you will be richly rewarded. A gift to a child is the most noble, most effective, longest lasting contribution that you can make to an individual and to the world. And

A Father Shares

you yourself will receive the most precious of dividends. Where but in your home will you find a community that will nurture and comfort you even when you don't deserve it, and remain caring and true no matter the circumstances? Your family will give you present joy and a treasure of memories to relish later.

Who said *"empty* nest"? Not me! With six children and two "adopted ones" continually reminding us of their love, and with two grandsons ripping through the house, trailed by an imitative little girl —well, *empty* scarcely fits.